Keto Diet Cookbook for Beginners UK

150 Budget-Friendly, Nutrient-Rich, and Tasty Ketogenic Recipes

Table of contents

Breakfasts to Kick-Start Your Keto Journey 7

   Chia Seed Pudding with Mixed Berries 7

   Cheesy Spinach and Mushroom Frittata..7

   Creamy Coconut and Almond Smoothie 8

   Keto Breakfast Burritos 8

   Classic Avocado and Bacon Omelette..9

   Almond Flour Pancakes with Blueberries 9

   Sausage and Egg Breakfast Casserole 10

   Keto Bagels with Cream Cheese and Salmon 10

   Full English Breakfast, Keto-Style 11

   Raspberry and Coconut Breakfast Parfait 11

   Smoked Mackerel and Scrambled Eggs 12

   Breakfast Sausage and Cheese Muffins...12

   Greek Yoghurt and Strawberry Smoothie Bowl...13

   Savoury Breakfast Stuffed Peppers 13

   Zucchini and Feta Breakfast Muffins 14

Hearty and Satisfying Keto Lunches 15

   Caprese Salad with Avocado 15

   Creamy Chicken Salad Wraps...15

   Mediterranean Zucchini Noodles 16

   Cauliflower Fried Rice with Shrimp 16

   Egg Salad Stuffed Avocado...17

   Spaghetti Squash Carbonara 17

   Bacon and Blue Cheese Stuffed Burgers 18

   Sesame Chicken Salad with Cucumber 18

   Keto Tuna Salad with Capers and Olives 19

   Greek Salad with Grilled Halloumi 19

   Creamy Spinach and Artichoke Dip 20

   Broccoli, Cheddar, and Ham Soup 20

   Stuffed Portobello Mushrooms with Feta...21

   Prawn and Avocado Lettuce Wraps 21

   Grilled Asparagus and Prosciutto Salad 22

Dinner Ideas: Low-Carb, High Flavour...23

   Lemon Butter Chicken Thighs 23

   Pan-seared Salmon with Asparagus 23

   Garlic Butter Steak Bites 24

   Keto Butter Chicken Curry..24

   Stuffed Pork Chops with Mozzarella and Spinach 25

   Grilled Lamb Chops with Rosemary 25

   Balsamic Glazed Chicken and Veggies...26

Thai Basil Beef Stir-fry 26

Sausage and Cabbage Skillet 27

Creamy Cajun Shrimp and Sausage Pasta 27

Eggplant Parmesan Casserole 28

Beef and Broccoli Stir-fry 28

Stuffed Bell Peppers with Ground Turkey 29

Lemon Herb Roasted Chicken 29

Zucchini Lasagna with Beef and Ricotta 30

Keto-Friendly Fish and Seafood Dishes 31

Garlic Butter Shrimp Scampi 31

Grilled Swordfish Steaks with Salsa Verde 31

Lemon-Dill Baked Salmon 32

Crab Stuffed Avocado 32

Grilled Tuna Steaks with Chimichurri 33

Keto Lobster Bisque 33

Spicy Tuna Avocado Boats 34

Seared Scallops with Brown Butter Sauce 34

Lemon-Parsley Baked Cod 35

Cilantro Lime Shrimp with Zucchini Noodles 35

Creamy Clam Chowder 36

Grilled Sardines with Garlic and Lemon 36

Keto Seafood Gumbo 37

Baked Trout with Almond Pesto 37

Sared Mackerel with Green Beans 38

Delicious Keto Meat and Poultry Recipes 39

Balsamic Glazed Pork Chops 39

Garlic Herb Lamb Chops 39

Chicken Tikka Masala 40

Rosemary Roasted Turkey Breast 40

Keto Beef Stroganoff 41

Lemon-Thyme Roasted Chicken 41

Bacon-Wrapped Filet Mignon 42

Creamy Tuscan Garlic Chicken 42

Grilled Moroccan Lamb Kebabs 43

Garlic Parmesan Crusted Pork Tenderloin 43

Bacon-Wrapped Stuffed Chicken 44

Slow Cooker Keto Pulled Pork 44

Cajun Chicken Alfredo 45

Baked Lemon Herb Chicken Thighs 45

Herb-Crusted Rack of Lamb 46

Vegetarian and Vegan Options on Keto 47

Spinach and Feta Stuffed Portobello Mushrooms 47

Cheesy Cauliflower Bake 47

Keto Eggplant Parmesan 48

Zucchini Noodles with Pesto and Sun-dried Tomatoes...48

Creamy Avocado Spinach Spaghetti Squash..49

Roasted Red Pepper and Tomato Soup 49

Vegan Keto Thai Curry 50

Cauliflower Tabbouleh Salad 50

Vegan Keto Pad Thai..51

Avocado and Walnut Salad 51

Spinach and Artichoke Dip 52

Vegan Keto Coconut Curry 52

Creamy Vegan Broccoli Soup 53

Vegan Stuffed Bell Peppers...53

Marinated Grilled Eggplant 54

Soups, Salads, and Sides: Perfect Keto Companions 55

Creamy Cauliflower Soup 55

Spinach, Bacon, and Egg Salad 55

Parmesan Roasted Brussels Sprouts..56

Greek Tzatziki Cucumber Salad...56

Roasted Garlic Mashed Cauliflower..57

Zucchini and Parmesan Fritters 57

Creamy Keto Coleslaw 58

Asparagus and Prosciutto Bundles 58

Keto Italian Antipasto Salad..59

Lemon Herb Roasted Asparagus 59

Bacon, Cheddar, and Chive Deviled Eggs 60

Loaded Keto Cauliflower Casserole...60

Avocado and Bacon Spinach Salad 61

Cheesy Keto Garlic Breadsticks 61

Creamy Cucumber Dill Salad...62

Keto Comfort Foods: British Classics Reimagined 63

Keto Cottage Pie..63

Keto Yorkshire Puddings 63

Cauliflower Cheese Soup 64

Keto Bangers and Mash...64

Keto Beef and Ale Stew 65

Keto Toad in the Hole 65

Cauliflower Shepherd's Pie..66

Keto Bubble and Squeak 66

Keto Ploughman's Lunch...67

Keto Chicken Tikka Masala 67

Keto Eton Mess 68

Keto Cornish Pasties 68

Keto Full English Breakfast 69

Keto Steak and Kidney Pie 69

Keto Fish and Chips with Tartar Sauce 70

Desserts for the Sweet-Toothed Keto Enthusiast 71

Chocolate Avocado Mousse 71

Raspberry Keto Cheesecake 71

Keto Lemon Curd Tart 72

Keto Chocolate Chip Cookies 72

Keto Tiramisu 73

Keto Chocolate Almond Bark 73

Keto Strawberry Shortcake 74

Keto Panna Cotta with Mixed Berries 74

Keto Chocolate Lava Cake 75

Keto Key Lime Pie 76

Keto Blueberry Muffins 76

Keto Brownies with Walnuts 77

Keto Vanilla Custard 77

Keto Cinnamon Rolls 78

Keto Coconut Cream Pie 79

Homemade Keto Snacks for On-the-Go 80

Keto Almond Joy Bites 80

Keto Pork Rinds 80

Keto Avocado Hummus 81

Keto Pizza Rolls 81

Keto Parmesan Crisps 82

Keto Buffalo Chicken Dip 82

Keto Garlic Herb Crackers 83

Keto Cucumber Bites with Smoked Salmon 83

Keto Mozzarella Sticks 84

Keto Coconut Almond Bars 84

Keto Guacamole and Flaxseed Crackers 85

Keto Greek Tzatziki Dip 85

Keto Peanut Butter Cups 86

Keto Jalapeno Poppers 86

Keto Olive Tapenade with Zucchini Chips 87

Breakfasts to Kick-Start Your Keto Journey

Chia Seed Pudding with Mixed Berries
Yield: 4 servings | Prep time: 15 minutes | Cook time: 0 minutes

Ingredients:

- 60 grams chia seeds
- 240 milliliters unsweetened coconut milk
- 10 grams erythritol or other keto-friendly sweetener
- 5 milliliters pure vanilla extract
- Pinch of salt
- 100 grams mixed berries (strawberries, raspberries, blueberries, and blackberries)

Directions:

1. In a mixing bowl, combine the chia seeds, coconut milk, erythritol, vanilla extract, and a pinch of salt. Stir well to combine.
2. Cover the bowl with plastic wrap or a lid and refrigerate for at least 3 hours or overnight. The chia seeds will absorb the liquid and create a thick pudding-like texture.
3. Before serving, give the pudding a good stir to break up any clumps. If the pudding is too thick, you can add a little more coconut milk to reach your desired consistency.
4. Divide the pudding into four servings and top with mixed berries.
5. Serve chilled.

Nutritional Information: Estimated per serving: 173 calories, 3 grams protein, 6 grams carbohydrates, 14 grams fat, 8 grams fiber, 0 milligrams cholesterol, 45 milligrams sodium, 98 milligrams potassium.

Cheesy Spinach and Mushroom Frittata
Yield: 4 servings | Prep time: 10 minutes | Cook time: 20 minutes

Ingredients:

- 8 large eggs
- 120 milliliters heavy cream
- 100 grams grated cheddar cheese
- 200 grams fresh spinach, chopped
- 200 grams mushrooms, sliced
- 1 small onion, diced (optional, omit for lower carbs)
- 30 milliliters olive oil
- Salt and pepper to taste

Directions:

1. Preheat your oven to 180°C (350°F).
2. In a large oven-safe skillet, heat the olive oil over medium heat. Add the mushrooms and onions (if using) and sauté until softened, about 5 minutes. Add the chopped spinach and cook for an additional 2 minutes until wilted.
3. In a large mixing bowl, whisk together the eggs, heavy cream, half of the cheddar cheese, salt, and pepper.
4. Pour the egg mixture into the skillet with the vegetables, ensuring an even distribution of ingredients. Cook for 2-3 minutes until the edges begin to set.
5. Sprinkle the remaining cheddar cheese on top of the frittata. Transfer the skillet to the preheated oven and bake for 12-15 minutes, or until the frittata is set in the middle and the cheese is melted and golden brown.
6. Remove from the oven and let it cool for a few minutes before slicing and serving.

Nutritional Information: Estimated per serving: 375 calories, 22 grams protein, 5 grams carbohydrates, 30 grams fat, 1 gram fiber, 387 milligrams cholesterol, 340 milligrams sodium, 375 milligrams potassium.

Creamy Coconut and Almond Smoothie

Yield: 2 servings | Prep time: 5 minutes | Cook time: 0 minutes

Ingredients:

- 240 milliliters unsweetened coconut milk
- 60 milliliters heavy cream
- 30 grams almond butter
- 1 tablespoon chia seeds
- 10 grams erythritol or other keto-friendly sweetener
- 5 milliliters vanilla extract
- A pinch of salt
- Ice cubes (optional)

Directions:

1. In a blender, combine the coconut milk, heavy cream, almond butter, chia seeds, erythritol, vanilla extract, and salt. Blend until smooth and creamy.
2. If you prefer a colder smoothie, add a few ice cubes to the blender and blend until the ice is crushed and the smoothie is chilled.
3. Pour the smoothie into two glasses and serve immediately. You can optionally garnish with some shredded coconut or a sprinkle of chia seeds on top.

Nutritional Information: Estimated per serving: 314 calories, 4 grams protein, 6 grams carbohydrates, 30 grams fat, 4 grams fiber, 41 milligrams cholesterol, 55 milligrams sodium, 166 milligrams potassium.

Keto Breakfast Burritos

Yield: 4 servings | Prep time: 10 minutes | Cook time: 15 minutes

Ingredients:

- 4 large lettuce leaves or low-carb tortillas
- 8 large eggs
- 120 milliliters heavy cream
- 200 grams cooked bacon, crumbled
- 100 grams cheddar cheese, shredded
- 50 grams diced tomatoes
- 50 grams diced bell peppers
- 30 milliliters olive oil
- Salt and pepper to taste

Directions:

1. In a mixing bowl, whisk together the eggs, heavy cream, salt, and pepper.
2. Heat the olive oil in a large non-stick skillet over medium heat. Pour the egg mixture into the skillet and cook, stirring occasionally, until the eggs are scrambled and cooked through.
3. Remove the skillet from the heat and set aside.
4. Lay out the lettuce leaves or low-carb tortillas on a flat surface. Divide the scrambled eggs, crumbled bacon, shredded cheddar cheese, diced tomatoes, and diced bell peppers among the lettuce leaves or tortillas.
5. Roll each lettuce leaf or tortilla around the filling, tucking in the sides as you go, to form a burrito shape.
6. Serve the breakfast burritos immediately or wrap them in foil and store in the refrigerator for a quick on-the-go breakfast.

Nutritional Information: Estimated per serving: 532 calories, 28 grams protein, 5 grams carbohydrates, 44 grams fat, 1 gram fiber, 412 milligrams cholesterol, 827 milligrams sodium, 287 milligrams potassium.

Classic Avocado and Bacon Omelette
Yield: 2 servings | Prep time: 5 minutes | Cook time: 10 minutes

Ingredients:

- 4 large eggs
- 1 ripe avocado, pitted and sliced
- 4 strips of bacon
- 50 grams cheddar cheese, shredded
- 15 milliliters heavy cream
- Salt and pepper to taste
- 15 milliliters olive oil

Directions:

1. In a non-stick skillet, cook the bacon over medium heat until crispy. Remove the bacon from the skillet and drain it on paper towels. Once cooled, crumble or chop the bacon into small pieces.
2. In a bowl, whisk together the eggs, heavy cream, salt, and pepper until well combined.
3. Heat the olive oil in the same skillet over medium heat. Pour the egg mixture into the skillet and cook for 2-3 minutes, or until the edges of the omelette begin to set.
4. Sprinkle the crumbled bacon, avocado slices, and shredded cheddar cheese over one half of the omelette. Carefully fold the other half of the omelette over the filling.
5. Continue to cook the omelette for 2-3 minutes, or until the cheese is melted and the omelette is cooked through.
6. Slide the omelette onto a plate, cut it in half, and serve immediately.

Nutritional Information: Estimated per serving: 514 calories, 25 grams protein, 5 grams carbohydrates, 44 grams fat, 5 grams fiber, 394 milligrams cholesterol, 642 milligrams sodium, 532 milligrams potassium.

Almond Flour Pancakes with Blueberries
Yield: 4 servings | Prep time: 5 minutes | Cook time: 15 minutes

Ingredients:

- 150 grams almond flour
- 50 grams fresh blueberries
- 4 large eggs
- 60 milliliters heavy cream
- 10 grams erythritol or other keto-friendly sweetener
- 5 milliliters vanilla extract
- 2 grams baking powder
- A pinch of salt
- 15 milliliters coconut oil or butter, for frying

Directions:

1. In a large mixing bowl, combine the almond flour, erythritol, baking powder, and salt.
2. In a separate bowl, whisk together the eggs, heavy cream, and vanilla extract.
3. Pour the wet ingredients into the dry ingredients and stir until a smooth batter forms. Gently fold in the blueberries.
4. Heat a non-stick skillet over medium heat and add a small amount of coconut oil or butter.
5. Pour a small amount of batter into the skillet to form a pancake. Cook for 2-3 minutes on each side, or until the pancake is golden brown and cooked through.
6. Repeat with the remaining batter, adding more coconut oil or butter to the skillet as needed.
7. Serve the pancakes with additional blueberries and a dollop of whipped cream if desired.

Nutritional Information: Estimated per serving: 327 calories, 13 grams protein, 9 grams carbohydrates, 28 grams fat, 4 grams fiber, 193 milligrams cholesterol, 230 milligrams sodium, 204 milligrams potassium.

Sausage and Egg Breakfast Casserole
Yield: 6 servings | Prep time: 10 minutes | Cook time: 30 minutes

Ingredients:

- 500 grams pork sausages, casings removed
- 8 large eggs
- 200 milliliters heavy cream
- 200 grams cheddar cheese, shredded
- 1 medium onion, diced
- 2 cloves garlic, minced
- 100 grams spinach leaves
- 15 milliliters olive oil
- Salt and pepper to taste

Directions:

1. Preheat your oven to 180°C (350°F).
2. Heat the olive oil in a large skillet over medium heat. Add the onions and garlic, and sauté until softened, about 3 minutes.
3. Add the sausage to the skillet and cook, breaking it up with a spoon, until browned and cooked through.
4. Stir in the spinach leaves and cook until wilted. Remove the skillet from the heat.
5. In a large mixing bowl, whisk together the eggs, heavy cream, salt, and pepper.
6. Grease a baking dish with olive oil or butter. Layer the cooked sausage mixture at the bottom of the dish.
7. Pour the egg mixture over the sausage. Sprinkle the shredded cheddar cheese on top.
8. Bake in the preheated oven for 25-30 minutes, or until the casserole is set and the cheese is melted and lightly browned.
9. Remove from the oven and let it cool for a few minutes before slicing and serving.

Nutritional Information: Estimated per serving: 634 calories, 31 grams protein, 4 grams carbohydrates, 53 grams fat, 1 gram fiber, 346 milligrams cholesterol, 1052 milligrams sodium, 374 milligrams potassium.

Keto Bagels with Cream Cheese and Salmon
Yield: 4 servings | Prep time: 15 minutes | Cook time: 12 minutes

Ingredients:

For the bagels:
- 200 grams almond flour
- 75 grams mozzarella cheese, shredded
- 50 grams cream cheese
- 2 large eggs
- 10 grams baking powder
- 5 grams psyllium husk powder

- A pinch of salt

For the topping:
- 200 grams cream cheese, softened
- 150 grams smoked salmon
- Fresh dill, for garnish
- Black pepper, to taste

Directions:

1. Preheat your oven to 220°C (425°F). Line a baking tray with parchment paper.
2. In a microwave-safe bowl, combine the mozzarella cheese and cream cheese. Microwave for 1 minute, stir, and microwave for another 30 seconds until melted and smooth.
3. In a large mixing bowl, combine the almond flour, psyllium husk powder, baking powder, and salt. Add the melted cheese mixture and eggs. Mix until a dough forms.
4. Divide the dough into 4 equal portions. Shape each portion into a bagel shape and place them on the prepared baking tray.
5. Bake in the preheated oven for 10-12 minutes, or until the bagels are golden brown.
6. Let the bagels cool on the tray for a few minutes, then transfer them to a wire rack to cool completely.
7. Once cooled, slice each bagel in half. Spread a generous amount of cream cheese on each half, top with smoked salmon, and garnish with fresh dill and black pepper.

Nutritional Information: Estimated per serving: 567 calories, 29 grams protein, 8 grams carbohydrates, 47 grams fat, 4 grams fiber, 158 milligrams cholesterol, 1130 milligrams sodium, 309 milligrams potassium.

Full English Breakfast, Keto-Style

Yield: 4 servings | Prep time: 10 minutes | Cook time: 25 minutes

Ingredients:

- 4 large eggs
- 4 slices bacon
- 4 pork sausages
- 200 grams mushrooms, sliced
- 200 grams cherry tomatoes, halved
- 100 grams spinach leaves
- 2 tablespoons olive oil
- Salt and pepper to taste
- Optional: Hot sauce, for serving

Directions:

1. Preheat your oven to 200°C (400°F). Line a baking tray with parchment paper.
2. Place the sausages and bacon on the prepared baking tray. Bake in the preheated oven for 15-20 minutes, turning halfway through, until the bacon is crispy and the sausages are cooked through.
3. While the sausages and bacon are cooking, heat the olive oil in a large skillet over medium heat. Add the mushrooms and tomatoes, and season with salt and pepper. Cook for 5-7 minutes, stirring occasionally, until the vegetables are softened and browned.
4. Push the vegetables to the side of the skillet, add the spinach, and cook until wilted, about 2 minutes. Remove the skillet from the heat.
5. In another skillet, fry the eggs over medium heat until the whites are set but the yolks are still runny, about 3 minutes.
6. Divide the sausages, bacon, vegetables, and fried eggs among four plates. Season with additional salt and pepper if desired, and serve with hot sauce on the side.

Nutritional Information: Estimated per serving: 567 calories, 33 grams protein, 9 grams carbohydrates, 44 grams fat, 2 grams fiber, 239 milligrams cholesterol, 1180 milligrams sodium, 698 milligrams potassium.

Raspberry and Coconut Breakfast Parfait

Yield: 4 servings | Prep time: 10 minutes | Cook time: 0 minutes

Ingredients:

- 250 grams fresh raspberries
- 400 milliliters canned coconut milk (full fat)
- 2 tablespoons chia seeds
- 2 tablespoons desiccated coconut
- 2 tablespoons unsweetened shredded coconut
- 2 tablespoons erythritol (or preferred keto-friendly sweetener)
- 1 teaspoon vanilla extract

Directions:

1. In a medium-sized bowl, mix the coconut milk, chia seeds, desiccated coconut, erythritol, and vanilla extract until well combined. Allow the mixture to sit for about 10 minutes, stirring occasionally, until it thickens to a pudding-like consistency.
2. In four serving glasses, layer the raspberry and coconut mixture, alternating between the two. Start with a layer of raspberries at the bottom, followed by a layer of the coconut mixture. Repeat until all the ingredients are used up.
3. Garnish with a sprinkle of shredded coconut on top of each parfait.
4. Chill in the refrigerator for at least 30 minutes before serving.

Nutritional Information: Estimated per serving: 240 calories, 3 grams protein, 9 grams carbohydrates, 22 grams fat, 5 grams fiber, 0 milligrams cholesterol, 16 milligrams sodium, 238 milligrams potassium.

Smoked Mackerel and Scrambled Eggs
Yield: 2 servings | Prep time: 5 minutes | Cook time: 5 minutes

Ingredients:

- 200 grams smoked mackerel fillets
- 4 large eggs
- 50 milliliters heavy cream
- 2 tablespoons butter
- Salt and pepper to taste
- 2 tablespoons chopped fresh chives (optional)
- 1 tablespoon olive oil for drizzling (optional)

Directions:

1. In a medium non-stick skillet, melt the butter over medium heat.
2. While the butter is melting, beat the eggs in a bowl with the heavy cream, salt, and pepper.
3. Pour the egg mixture into the skillet and cook, stirring occasionally, until the eggs are just set but still slightly creamy.
4. Flake the smoked mackerel fillets with a fork, removing any bones if necessary, and add them to the skillet. Gently fold the mackerel into the scrambled eggs until evenly distributed.
5. Serve the scrambled eggs and mackerel onto plates. Garnish with chopped chives and a drizzle of olive oil, if desired.

Nutritional Information: Estimated per serving: 485 calories, 35 grams protein, 1 gram carbohydrates, 37 grams fat, 0 grams fiber, 320 milligrams cholesterol, 370 milligrams sodium, 600 milligrams potassium.

Breakfast Sausage and Cheese Muffins
Yield: 6 servings | Prep time: 15 minutes | Cook time: 25 minutes

Ingredients:

- 250 grams ground pork sausage
- 4 large eggs
- 150 milliliters heavy cream
- 200 grams grated cheddar cheese
- 1 teaspoon baking powder
- 1/2 teaspoon salt
- 1/4 teaspoon ground black pepper
- 2 tablespoons chopped fresh chives (optional)

Directions:

1. Preheat your oven to 180°C (350°F) and grease a 6-cup muffin tin.
2. In a large skillet over medium heat, cook the ground pork sausage, breaking it apart with a spatula, until browned and cooked through. Drain any excess grease and set aside.
3. In a large mixing bowl, whisk together the eggs, heavy cream, baking powder, salt, and pepper until well combined.
4. Stir in the cooked sausage and grated cheddar cheese until evenly distributed.
5. Divide the mixture among the muffin cups, filling each one nearly to the top.
6. Bake for 25 minutes, or until the tops are golden brown and a toothpick inserted into the center of a muffin comes out clean.
7. Let the muffins cool for a few minutes before removing them from the tin. Garnish with chopped chives if desired.

Nutritional Information: Estimated per serving: 340 calories, 19 grams protein, 3 grams carbohydrates, 28 grams fat, 0 grams fiber, 195 milligrams cholesterol, 720 milligrams sodium, 220 milligrams potassium.

Greek Yoghurt and Strawberry Smoothie Bowl

Yield: 2 servings | Prep time: 10 minutes | Cook time: 0 minutes

Ingredients:

- 250 grams full-fat Greek yoghurt
- 100 grams fresh strawberries
- 50 grams chia seeds
- 2 tablespoons erythritol (or other keto-friendly sweetener)
- 30 grams unsweetened desiccated coconut
- 50 milliliters unsweetened almond milk
- 2 tablespoons crushed almonds
- 1 teaspoon vanilla extract

Directions:

1. In a blender, combine the Greek yoghurt, strawberries, almond milk, vanilla extract, and erythritol. Blend until smooth.
2. Pour the smoothie into two bowls.
3. Top each bowl with chia seeds, desiccated coconut, and crushed almonds.
4. Optional: Garnish with a few fresh strawberry slices for extra flavor and presentation.
5. Serve immediately and enjoy.

Nutritional Information: Estimated per serving: 290 calories, 12 grams protein, 10 grams carbohydrates, 23 grams fat, 6 grams fiber, 10 milligrams cholesterol, 100 milligrams sodium, 300 milligrams potassium.

Savoury Breakfast Stuffed Peppers

Yield: 4 servings | Prep time: 15 minutes | Cook time: 30 minutes

Ingredients:

- 4 large bell peppers (any color)
- 250 grams breakfast sausage
- 100 grams full-fat cream cheese
- 100 grams grated cheddar cheese
- 4 large eggs
- 2 tablespoons chopped fresh chives
- 1/2 teaspoon salt
- 1/4 teaspoon black pepper
- 1 tablespoon olive oil

Directions:

1. Preheat your oven to 190°C (375°F).
2. Cut the tops off the bell peppers and remove the seeds and membranes. Lightly brush the outside of the peppers with olive oil.
3. In a skillet over medium heat, cook the breakfast sausage until browned and cooked through. Remove from heat and set aside.
4. In a mixing bowl, beat the cream cheese until smooth. Add the eggs, salt, and pepper, and mix until combined.
5. Stir in the cooked sausage and cheddar cheese.
6. Spoon the sausage and egg mixture into the prepared bell peppers.
7. Place the stuffed peppers in a baking dish and bake in the preheated oven for 25-30 minutes, or until the eggs are set and the peppers are tender.
8. Sprinkle the chopped chives on top of the peppers before serving.

Nutritional Information: Estimated per serving: 480 calories, 22 grams protein, 8 grams carbohydrates, 40 grams fat, 2 grams fiber, 250 milligrams cholesterol, 800 milligrams sodium, 500 milligrams potassium.

Zucchini and Feta Breakfast Muffins

Yield: 6 servings | Prep time: 10 minutes | Cook time: 20 minutes

Ingredients:

- 200 grams almond flour
- 1 teaspoon baking powder
- 1/2 teaspoon salt
- 1/4 teaspoon black pepper
- 3 large eggs

- 100 grams full-fat Greek yoghurt
- 100 grams feta cheese, crumbled
- 150 grams zucchini, grated
- 2 tablespoons fresh chives, chopped
- 2 tablespoons olive oil

Directions:

1. Preheat your oven to 180°C (350°F). Line a muffin tin with 6 silicone or paper liners.
2. In a large mixing bowl, combine the almond flour, baking powder, salt, and black pepper.
3. In a separate bowl, beat the eggs and then add the Greek yoghurt and olive oil. Mix until well combined.
4. Gradually add the wet ingredients to the dry ingredients and mix until just combined.
5. Stir in the crumbled feta cheese, grated zucchini, and chopped chives.
6. Spoon the batter into the prepared muffin tin, filling each cup nearly to the top.
7. Bake in the preheated oven for 20-25 minutes, or until the tops are golden and a toothpick inserted into the center of a muffin comes out clean.
8. Allow the muffins to cool for a few minutes in the tin before transferring them to a wire rack to cool completely.

Nutritional Information: Estimated per serving: 290 calories, 12 grams protein, 8 grams carbohydrates, 25 grams fat, 3 grams fiber, 115 milligrams cholesterol, 380 milligrams sodium, 200 milligrams potassium.

Hearty and Satisfying Keto Lunches

Caprese Salad with Avocado

Yield: 4 servings | Prep time: 10 minutes | Cook time: 0 minutes

Ingredients:

- 2 large ripe avocados, sliced
- 4 medium ripe tomatoes, sliced
- 200 grams fresh mozzarella cheese, sliced
- 20 grams fresh basil leaves
- 60 milliliters extra-virgin olive oil
- 15 milliliters balsamic vinegar
- Salt and black pepper, to taste

Directions:

1. Arrange the sliced avocados, tomatoes, and mozzarella cheese on a platter, alternating and overlapping them.
2. Tuck the fresh basil leaves in between the avocado, tomato, and mozzarella slices.
3. Drizzle the extra-virgin olive oil and balsamic vinegar over the salad.
4. Season with salt and black pepper to taste.
5. Serve immediately.

Nutritional Information: Estimated per serving: 400 calories, 12 grams protein, 8 grams carbohydrates, 36 grams fat, 6 grams fiber, 30 milligrams cholesterol, 300 milligrams sodium, 650 milligrams potassium.

Creamy Chicken Salad Wraps

Yield: 4 servings | Prep time: 15 minutes | Cook time: 0 minutes

Ingredients:

- 400 grams cooked chicken breast, chopped
- 100 grams mayonnaise
- 50 grams Greek yogurt
- 2 stalks celery, chopped
- 50 grams chopped red onion
- 25 grams chopped fresh parsley
- Salt and black pepper, to taste
- 4 large lettuce leaves (e.g., iceberg, romaine, or butterhead)

Directions:

1. In a large mixing bowl, combine the chopped chicken, mayonnaise, Greek yogurt, celery, red onion, and parsley. Mix well.
2. Season the chicken salad with salt and black pepper to taste. Stir until well combined.
3. Place a lettuce leaf on a plate and spoon a quarter of the chicken salad onto the center of the leaf.
4. Fold the sides of the lettuce leaf over the chicken salad, then roll the leaf from the bottom to the top to create a wrap.
5. Repeat with the remaining lettuce leaves and chicken salad.
6. Serve immediately or refrigerate until ready to eat.

Nutritional Information: Estimated per serving: 350 calories, 25 grams protein, 5 grams carbohydrates, 25 grams fat, 1 gram fiber, 75 milligrams cholesterol, 400 milligrams sodium, 300 milligrams potassium.

Mediterranean Zucchini Noodles
Yield: 4 servings | Prep time: 15 minutes | Cook time: 10 minutes

Ingredients:

- 4 medium zucchinis, spiralized into noodles
- 3 tablespoons olive oil
- 4 cloves garlic, minced
- 200 grams cherry tomatoes, halved
- 150 grams Kalamata olives, pitted and chopped
- 100 grams feta cheese, crumbled
- 25 grams fresh basil leaves, chopped
- Salt and black pepper, to taste
- 1 tablespoon lemon juice
- Optional: crushed red pepper flakes, to taste

Directions:

1. In a large nonstick skillet, heat 2 tablespoons of olive oil over medium heat. Add the minced garlic and sauté until fragrant, about 1 minute.
2. Add the spiralized zucchini noodles to the skillet and sauté for about 5 minutes, until slightly softened but still al dente.
3. Remove the zucchini noodles from the skillet and transfer them to a large bowl.
4. Add the halved cherry tomatoes, chopped olives, crumbled feta cheese, and chopped basil to the bowl with the zucchini noodles. Toss everything together gently.
5. Drizzle the remaining 1 tablespoon of olive oil and the lemon juice over the zucchini noodle mixture. Season with salt and black pepper to taste. If desired, add crushed red pepper flakes for a little heat.
6. Toss everything together once more to combine, and serve immediately.

Nutritional Information: Estimated per serving: 250 calories, 8 grams protein, 12 grams carbohydrates, 20 grams fat, 3 grams fiber, 25 milligrams cholesterol, 750 milligrams sodium, 500 milligrams potassium.

Cauliflower Fried Rice with Shrimp
Yield: 4 servings | Prep time: 15 minutes | Cook time: 10 minutes

Ingredients:

- 500 grams cauliflower, riced
- 200 grams shrimp, peeled and deveined
- 3 tablespoons olive oil
- 1 small onion, finely chopped
- 2 cloves garlic, minced
- 100 grams frozen peas and carrots mix, thawed
- 2 large eggs, lightly beaten
- 3 tablespoons soy sauce (or tamari for gluten-free)
- 2 green onions, sliced
- Salt and black pepper, to taste

Directions:

1. Heat 1 tablespoon of olive oil in a large nonstick skillet over medium-high heat. Add the shrimp and cook until pink and opaque, about 3-4 minutes per side. Remove the shrimp from the skillet and set aside.
2. In the same skillet, heat 1 tablespoon of olive oil over medium heat. Add the chopped onion and sauté until translucent, about 2 minutes. Add the minced garlic and sauté for another minute.
3. Stir in the riced cauliflower and cook for about 5 minutes, until the cauliflower is tender but not mushy.
4. Push the cauliflower rice mixture to the side of the skillet. Add the remaining tablespoon of olive oil to the empty side of the skillet. Pour in the beaten eggs and scramble until just cooked through. Mix the scrambled eggs into the cauliflower rice.
5. Add the cooked shrimp, thawed peas and carrots mix, and soy sauce to the skillet. Stir to combine everything well. Season with salt and black pepper to taste.
6. Garnish with sliced green onions and serve immediately.

Nutritional Information: Estimated per serving: 250 calories, 15 grams protein, 15 grams carbohydrates, 15 grams fat, 5 grams fiber, 150 milligrams cholesterol, 800 milligrams sodium, 450 milligrams potassium.

Egg Salad Stuffed Avocado

Yield: 4 servings | Prep time: 15 minutes | Cook time: 10 minutes

Ingredients:

- 4 large eggs
- 2 ripe avocados
- 60 grams mayonnaise
- 1 tablespoon Dijon mustard
- 1 tablespoon fresh dill, chopped
- 1 tablespoon fresh parsley, chopped
- 1 tablespoon fresh chives, chopped
- 1 tablespoon lemon juice
- Salt and black pepper, to taste
- Paprika, for garnish

Directions:

1. Place the eggs in a medium saucepan and cover with cold water. Bring the water to a boil, then reduce the heat to low and simmer for 10 minutes. Remove from heat and immediately transfer the eggs to a bowl of ice water to cool. Once cooled, peel the eggs and chop them.
2. In a medium bowl, combine the chopped eggs, mayonnaise, Dijon mustard, dill, parsley, chives, lemon juice, salt, and black pepper. Stir well to combine.
3. Cut the avocados in half and remove the pits. Scoop out a bit of the avocado flesh to create a larger well for the egg salad, if needed. Spoon the egg salad mixture into the avocado halves.
4. Garnish with a sprinkle of paprika and additional fresh herbs, if desired. Serve immediately.

Nutritional Information: Estimated per serving: 310 calories, 10 grams protein, 8 grams carbohydrates, 28 grams fat, 7 grams fiber, 190 milligrams cholesterol, 310 milligrams sodium, 600 milligrams potassium.

Spaghetti Squash Carbonara

Yield: 4 servings | Prep time: 10 minutes | Cook time: 40 minutes

Ingredients:

- 1 medium spaghetti squash (about 1 kg)
- 100 grams pancetta or bacon, diced
- 2 large eggs
- 50 grams grated Parmesan cheese
- 50 grams grated Pecorino Romano cheese
- 2 cloves garlic, minced
- Salt and black pepper, to taste
- Fresh parsley, chopped, for garnish

Directions:

1. Preheat the oven to 200°C. Cut the spaghetti squash in half lengthwise and remove the seeds. Place the halves cut-side down on a baking sheet and bake for 30-40 minutes, or until the flesh is easily pierced with a fork. Let it cool for a few minutes, then use a fork to scrape out the spaghetti-like strands. Set aside.
2. In a large skillet over medium heat, cook the pancetta or bacon until crispy. Remove from the skillet and set aside. Leave the fat in the skillet.
3. In a medium bowl, whisk together the eggs, Parmesan, Pecorino Romano, and a pinch of black pepper. Set aside.
4. In the same skillet, add the garlic and sauté for 1-2 minutes until fragrant. Add the cooked spaghetti squash and toss to coat with the garlic. Remove from heat.
5. Quickly pour the egg and cheese mixture into the skillet and toss to combine. The heat from the squash will cook the eggs and create a creamy sauce. Add the pancetta or bacon and toss again.
6. Season with salt and black pepper to taste. Garnish with chopped parsley and serve immediately.

Nutritional Information: Estimated per serving: 250 calories, 13 grams protein, 15 grams carbohydrates, 17 grams fat, 3 grams fiber, 110 milligrams cholesterol, 490 milligrams sodium, 420 milligrams potassium.

Bacon and Blue Cheese Stuffed Burgers

Yield: 4 servings | Prep time: 10 minutes | Cook time: 15 minutes

Ingredients:

- 800 grams ground beef
- 100 grams blue cheese, crumbled
- 4 slices bacon, cooked and crumbled
- 1/2 teaspoon salt
- 1/4 teaspoon black pepper
- 1/2 teaspoon garlic powder
- 1/2 teaspoon onion powder
- 4 large lettuce leaves (for serving)
- 1 small red onion, sliced (optional, for serving)
- 1 tomato, sliced (optional, for serving)
- 1 avocado, sliced (optional, for serving)
- 1 tablespoon olive oil, for grilling

Directions:

1. Preheat your grill or stovetop pan over medium-high heat and lightly oil with olive oil.
2. In a large bowl, mix the ground beef with salt, black pepper, garlic powder, and onion powder. Divide the meat into 8 equal portions and shape each into a thin patty.
3. Place a spoonful of blue cheese and a sprinkle of bacon crumbles in the center of 4 of the patties. Top with the remaining 4 patties and press the edges to seal the stuffing inside.
4. Grill the burgers for 5-7 minutes per side, or until cooked to your desired level of doneness.
5. Serve the burgers wrapped in lettuce leaves and top with sliced onion, tomato, and avocado if desired.

Nutritional Information: Estimated per serving: 680 calories, 42 grams protein, 5 grams carbohydrates, 54 grams fat, 2 grams fiber, 150 milligrams cholesterol, 950 milligrams sodium, 520 milligrams potassium.

Sesame Chicken Salad with Cucumber

Yield: 4 servings | Prep time: 15 minutes | Cook time: 15 minutes

Ingredients:

- 500 grams chicken breasts, boneless and skinless
- 1 tablespoon sesame oil
- 1 tablespoon olive oil
- 2 medium cucumbers, sliced
- 4 tablespoons sesame seeds, toasted
- 1 teaspoon garlic powder
- 1 teaspoon onion powder
- Salt and pepper, to taste
- 4 tablespoons soy sauce (or tamari for gluten-free)
- 1 tablespoon rice vinegar
- 2 teaspoons erythritol or other keto-friendly sweetener
- 1 teaspoon ginger, minced
- 2 tablespoons green onions, chopped
- Mixed salad greens, for serving

Directions:

1. Heat the olive oil in a pan over medium heat. Season the chicken breasts with garlic powder, onion powder, salt, and pepper. Cook the chicken breasts in the pan for about 7-8 minutes on each side, or until fully cooked through. Let them rest for a few minutes, then slice into thin strips.
2. In a small bowl, whisk together the soy sauce, rice vinegar, erythritol, ginger, and half of the sesame seeds.
3. In a large bowl, toss the sliced cucumbers, chicken strips, and salad greens with the dressing.
4. Serve the salad in individual bowls, sprinkled with the remaining toasted sesame seeds and green onions. Drizzle with the sesame oil just before serving.

Nutritional Information: Estimated per serving: 340 calories, 33 grams protein, 7 grams carbohydrates, 20 grams fat, 2 grams fiber, 80 milligrams cholesterol, 980 milligrams sodium, 520 milligrams potassium.

Keto Tuna Salad with Capers and Olives

Yield: 4 servings | Prep time: 15 minutes | Cook time: 0 minutes

Ingredients:

- 2 cans (280 grams drained weight) tuna in olive oil, drained
- 50 grams capers, drained
- 70 grams black olives, pitted and chopped
- 70 grams green olives, pitted and chopped
- 1 small red onion, finely chopped
- 2 tablespoons olive oil
- 1 tablespoon apple cider vinegar
- 1 teaspoon Dijon mustard
- Salt and pepper, to taste
- Mixed salad greens, for serving

Directions:

1. In a large mixing bowl, combine the drained tuna, capers, chopped black and green olives, and chopped red onion.
2. In a small bowl, whisk together the olive oil, apple cider vinegar, Dijon mustard, salt, and pepper. Pour the dressing over the tuna mixture and toss to combine.
3. Serve the tuna salad on a bed of mixed salad greens.

Nutritional Information: Estimated per serving: 240 calories, 25 grams protein, 4 grams carbohydrates, 14 grams fat, 2 grams fiber, 30 milligrams cholesterol, 850 milligrams sodium, 310 milligrams potassium.

Greek Salad with Grilled Halloumi

Yield: 4 servings | Prep time: 15 minutes | Cook time: 5 minutes

Ingredients:

- 250 grams halloumi cheese, sliced
- 200 grams cherry tomatoes, halved
- 1 large cucumber, diced
- 1 large red onion, thinly sliced
- 150 grams Kalamata olives, pitted
- 100 grams feta cheese, crumbled
- 4 tablespoons extra virgin olive oil
- 2 tablespoons red wine vinegar
- 1 teaspoon dried oregano
- Salt and pepper, to taste
- Fresh basil leaves, for garnish

Directions:

1. Preheat a grill or grill pan over medium-high heat. Once hot, grill the halloumi slices for 1-2 minutes on each side until they have grill marks and are slightly softened. Remove from heat and set aside.
2. In a large salad bowl, combine the cherry tomatoes, cucumber, red onion, olives, and feta cheese.
3. In a small bowl, whisk together the olive oil, red wine vinegar, oregano, salt, and pepper. Drizzle the dressing over the salad and toss to combine.
4. Serve the salad in individual bowls, topped with grilled halloumi and garnished with fresh basil leaves.

Nutritional Information: Estimated per serving: 350 calories, 16 grams protein, 9 grams carbohydrates, 29 grams fat, 3 grams fiber, 60 milligrams cholesterol, 1,350 milligrams sodium, 330 milligrams potassium.

Creamy Spinach and Artichoke Dip
Yield: 6 servings | Prep time: 10 minutes | Cook time: 25 minutes

Ingredients:

- 200 grams frozen spinach, thawed and drained
- 200 grams canned artichoke hearts, drained and chopped
- 200 grams cream cheese, softened
- 100 grams sour cream
- 100 grams mayonnaise
- 100 grams grated Parmesan cheese
- 100 grams shredded mozzarella cheese
- 3 cloves garlic, minced
- 1/2 teaspoon crushed red pepper flakes (optional)
- Salt and pepper, to taste

Directions:

1. Preheat your oven to 190°C (375°F).
2. In a medium-sized mixing bowl, combine the cream cheese, sour cream, mayonnaise, and half of the Parmesan cheese. Mix until smooth and creamy.
3. Add the spinach, artichoke hearts, mozzarella cheese, garlic, red pepper flakes (if using), salt, and pepper to the bowl. Mix until all the ingredients are well incorporated.
4. Transfer the mixture to an oven-safe dish and spread it out evenly. Sprinkle the remaining Parmesan cheese on top.
5. Bake in the preheated oven for 20-25 minutes, or until the dip is bubbly and the top is golden brown.
6. Allow the dip to cool for a few minutes before serving. Serve with vegetable sticks, pork rinds, or keto-friendly crackers.

Nutritional Information: Estimated per serving: 370 calories, 11 grams protein, 5 grams carbohydrates, 35 grams fat, 2 grams fiber, 90 milligrams cholesterol, 640 milligrams sodium, 220 milligrams potassium.

Broccoli, Cheddar, and Ham Soup
Yield: 4 servings | Prep time: 10 minutes | Cook time: 25 minutes

Ingredients:

- 400 grams broccoli, chopped into florets
- 200 grams ham, diced
- 200 grams cheddar cheese, shredded
- 50 grams butter
- 1 small onion, diced
- 2 cloves garlic, minced
- 400 milliliters chicken broth
- 200 milliliters heavy cream
- 1/2 teaspoon mustard powder
- 1/2 teaspoon paprika
- Salt and pepper, to taste

Directions:

1. In a large saucepan, melt the butter over medium heat. Add the diced onion and cook for 3-4 minutes, or until it becomes translucent. Add the minced garlic and cook for an additional 1-2 minutes.
2. Pour in the chicken broth and bring it to a simmer. Add the broccoli florets and cook for 5-7 minutes, or until they are tender.
3. Using an immersion blender, partially blend the soup, leaving some chunks of broccoli. Alternatively, you can transfer some of the soup to a regular blender, blend, and then return it to the pot.
4. Add the diced ham, heavy cream, mustard powder, paprika, salt, and pepper. Stir until well combined and heated through.
5. Gradually add the shredded cheddar cheese, stirring continuously until the cheese has melted and the soup is creamy.
6. Serve hot, with additional shredded cheese on top if desired.

Nutritional Information: Estimated per serving: 530 calories, 23 grams protein, 10 grams carbohydrates, 44 grams fat, 2 grams fiber, 130 milligrams cholesterol, 1100 milligrams sodium, 550 milligrams potassium.

Stuffed Portobello Mushrooms with Feta

Yield: 4 servings | Prep time: 10 minutes | Cook time: 20 minutes

Ingredients:

- 4 large portobello mushrooms (approximately 400 grams)
- 200 grams feta cheese, crumbled
- 100 grams spinach, finely chopped
- 1 small onion, finely diced
- 2 cloves garlic, minced
- 2 tablespoons olive oil
- 2 tablespoons fresh basil, chopped
- 1/2 teaspoon dried oregano
- Salt and pepper, to taste

Directions:

1. Preheat your oven to 200°C (400°F).
2. Clean the portobello mushrooms by gently wiping them with a damp cloth. Remove the stems and gills from the mushrooms.
3. In a small pan, heat 1 tablespoon of olive oil over medium heat. Add the diced onion and sauté until translucent. Add the garlic and cook for an additional 1-2 minutes.
4. Add the chopped spinach to the pan and cook until wilted. Remove from heat and set aside.
5. In a mixing bowl, combine the crumbled feta cheese, sautéed onion, garlic, spinach, chopped basil, dried oregano, salt, and pepper.
6. Brush the outside of the portobello mushrooms with the remaining 1 tablespoon of olive oil and place them on a baking tray, gill-side up. Divide the feta mixture among the mushrooms, pressing down to fill the cavities.
7. Bake in the preheated oven for 15-20 minutes, or until the mushrooms are tender and the filling is heated through.
8. Serve immediately.

Nutritional Information: Estimated per serving: 230 calories, 9 grams protein, 7 grams carbohydrates, 18 grams fat, 2 grams fiber, 30 milligrams cholesterol, 600 milligrams sodium, 450 milligrams potassium.

Prawn and Avocado Lettuce Wraps

Yield: 4 servings | Prep time: 15 minutes | Cook time: 5 minutes

Ingredients:

- 200 grams cooked prawns, shelled and deveined
- 2 ripe avocados, diced
- 1 small red onion, finely chopped
- 2 medium tomatoes, diced
- 1 small red chilli, deseeded and finely chopped
- 1 clove garlic, minced
- 1 lime, juiced
- 1 tablespoon olive oil
- 1 tablespoon fresh coriander, chopped
- Salt and pepper, to taste
- 8 large lettuce leaves (e.g., iceberg or romaine)

Directions:

1. In a medium bowl, combine prawns, avocados, red onion, tomatoes, red chilli, garlic, lime juice, olive oil, and coriander. Mix gently until all ingredients are well combined. Season with salt and pepper to taste.
2. Rinse and pat dry the lettuce leaves. Select the most sturdy and whole leaves.
3. Spoon the prawn and avocado mixture onto each lettuce leaf, dividing the mixture evenly among the wraps.
4. Serve immediately, using the lettuce leaves to wrap around the filling. Enjoy as a light, refreshing, and low-carb meal or snack.

Nutritional Information: Estimated per serving: 235 calories, 12 grams protein, 9 grams carbohydrates, 17 grams fat, 6 grams fiber, 85 milligrams cholesterol, 285 milligrams sodium, 645 milligrams potassium.

Grilled Asparagus and Prosciutto Salad

Yield: 4 servings | Prep time: 10 minutes | Cook time: 10 minutes

Ingredients:

- 400 grams asparagus spears, trimmed
- 120 grams prosciutto
- 2 tablespoons olive oil
- Salt and pepper, to taste
- 60 grams rocket (arugula) leaves
- 50 grams Parmesan cheese, shaved
- 1 tablespoon balsamic vinegar
- 1 tablespoon extra virgin olive oil

Directions:

1. Preheat a grill or barbecue to medium-high heat.
2. Toss the asparagus spears in the 2 tablespoons of olive oil and season with salt and pepper.
3. Place the asparagus on the hot grill and cook for about 5 minutes, turning occasionally, until they are lightly charred and tender. Remove from the grill and set aside.
4. Arrange the rocket leaves on a serving platter. Top with the grilled asparagus and prosciutto. Sprinkle over the shaved Parmesan cheese.
5. In a small bowl, whisk together the balsamic vinegar and extra virgin olive oil. Drizzle the dressing over the salad.
6. Serve immediately as a light and flavorful appetizer or side dish.

Nutritional Information: Estimated per serving: 235 calories, 11 grams protein, 4 grams carbohydrates, 20 grams fat, 2 grams fiber, 20 milligrams cholesterol, 600 milligrams sodium, 250 milligrams potassium.

Dinner Ideas: Low-Carb, High Flavour

Lemon Butter Chicken Thighs

Yield: 4 servings | Prep time: 10 minutes | Cook time: 25 minutes

Ingredients:

- 4 bone-in, skin-on chicken thighs (about 600 grams)
- Salt and pepper, to taste
- 2 tablespoons olive oil
- 4 cloves garlic, minced
- 100 milliliters chicken stock
- Juice of 2 lemons (about 80 milliliters)
- 60 grams unsalted butter, cut into cubes
- 2 tablespoons fresh parsley, chopped

Directions:

1. Preheat your oven to 200°C (180°C fan-forced).
2. Season the chicken thighs with salt and pepper on both sides.
3. In an ovenproof skillet or frying pan, heat the olive oil over medium-high heat. Add the chicken thighs, skin-side down, and cook for 5 minutes until the skin is golden brown and crispy. Turn the thighs over and cook for another 3 minutes. Remove the chicken from the skillet and set aside.
4. In the same skillet, add the minced garlic and cook for about 1 minute until fragrant. Pour in the chicken stock and lemon juice, scraping up any browned bits from the bottom of the skillet. Bring to a simmer and cook for 2 minutes.
5. Add the butter to the skillet and stir until melted. Return the chicken thighs to the skillet, skin-side up.
6. Transfer the skillet to the preheated oven and bake for 15 minutes, or until the chicken is cooked through and the internal temperature reaches 74°C.
7. Remove from the oven, sprinkle with chopped parsley, and serve.

Nutritional Information: Estimated per serving: 420 calories, 27 grams protein, 3 grams carbohydrates, 34 grams fat, 0 grams fiber, 150 milligrams cholesterol, 300 milligrams sodium, 250 milligrams potassium.

Pan-seared Salmon with Asparagus

Yield: 4 servings | Prep time: 10 minutes | Cook time: 15 minutes

Ingredients:

- 4 salmon fillets, skin-on (about 600 grams total)
- Salt and pepper, to taste
- 2 tablespoons olive oil
- 1 bunch of asparagus, trimmed (about 250 grams)
- 3 cloves garlic, minced
- Zest and juice of 1 lemon (about 30 milliliters juice)
- 2 tablespoons unsalted butter

Directions:

1. Season the salmon fillets with salt and pepper on both sides.
2. Heat 1 tablespoon of olive oil in a large non-stick skillet over medium-high heat. Add the salmon fillets, skin-side down, and cook for 4-5 minutes until the skin is crispy. Turn the fillets over and cook for an additional 3-4 minutes, or until the salmon is cooked to your desired level of doneness. Remove the salmon from the skillet and set aside.
3. In the same skillet, add the remaining 1 tablespoon of olive oil and the asparagus. Cook for 3-4 minutes, or until the asparagus is tender-crisp. Add the minced garlic and cook for an additional 1 minute until fragrant.
4. Add the lemon zest, lemon juice, and butter to the skillet. Stir until the butter is melted and the asparagus is coated in the sauce.
5. Serve the salmon fillets with the asparagus, drizzling any remaining sauce from the skillet over the top.

Nutritional Information: Estimated per serving: 370 calories, 33 grams protein, 5 grams carbohydrates, 24 grams fat, 2 grams fiber, 95 milligrams cholesterol, 200 milligrams sodium, 600 milligrams potassium.

Garlic Butter Steak Bites
Yield: 4 servings | Prep time: 10 minutes | Cook time: 10 minutes

Ingredients:

- 500 grams sirloin steak, cut into bite-sized cubes
- Salt and pepper, to taste
- 2 tablespoons olive oil
- 5 cloves garlic, minced
- 50 grams unsalted butter
- 2 tablespoons chopped fresh parsley

Directions:

1. Season the steak bites with salt and pepper.
2. Heat 1 tablespoon of olive oil in a large skillet over medium-high heat. Add half of the steak bites and sear them until browned on all sides, about 3-4 minutes. Remove the steak bites from the skillet and set them aside. Repeat with the remaining steak bites and olive oil.
3. Reduce the heat to medium and add the minced garlic to the skillet. Cook for about 1 minute, or until the garlic is fragrant.
4. Add the butter to the skillet and stir until it's melted. Return the steak bites to the skillet and toss them in the garlic butter until they're well-coated.
5. Remove the skillet from the heat and sprinkle the steak bites with chopped parsley.
6. Serve the steak bites as an appetizer, or as a main dish with your favourite keto-friendly sides.

Nutritional Information: Estimated per serving: 410 calories, 32 grams protein, 1 gram carbohydrates, 30 grams fat, 0 grams fiber, 115 milligrams cholesterol, 220 milligrams sodium, 430 milligrams potassium.

Keto Butter Chicken Curry
Yield: 4 servings | Prep time: 15 minutes | Cook time: 30 minutes

Ingredients:

- 500 grams boneless, skinless chicken thighs, cubed
- Salt and pepper, to taste
- 2 tablespoons ghee or unsalted butter
- 1 medium onion, finely chopped
- 4 cloves garlic, minced
- 1 tablespoon grated fresh ginger
- 1 tablespoon ground turmeric
- 1 tablespoon ground cumin
- 1 tablespoon ground coriander
- 1 teaspoon chili powder
- 1 teaspoon paprika
- 1 teaspoon ground cinnamon
- 400 grams canned tomatoes, diced
- 200 ml coconut cream
- 2 tablespoons fresh cilantro, chopped

Directions:

1. Season the chicken cubes with salt and pepper.
2. Heat ghee or butter in a large skillet over medium-high heat. Add the chicken cubes and brown them on all sides. Remove from the skillet and set aside.
3. In the same skillet, add the chopped onions and sauté until they're translucent, about 5 minutes. Add the garlic and ginger and continue sautéing for another 2 minutes.
4. Add the ground spices (turmeric, cumin, coriander, chili powder, paprika, cinnamon) to the skillet and cook for another 2 minutes, stirring constantly, until the spices are fragrant.
5. Return the browned chicken to the skillet, add the canned tomatoes and bring to a simmer. Reduce the heat to low, cover and let simmer for 20 minutes.
6. Stir in the coconut cream and simmer for an additional 5 minutes. Season to taste with additional salt and pepper.
7. Serve the curry over cauliflower rice or your favorite keto-friendly side. Garnish with chopped fresh cilantro.

Nutritional Information: Estimated per serving: 485 calories, 29 grams protein, 12 grams carbohydrates, 36 grams fat, 4 grams fiber, 115 milligrams cholesterol, 560 milligrams sodium, 840 milligrams potassium.

Stuffed Pork Chops with Mozzarella and Spinach

Yield: 4 servings | Prep time: 10 minutes | Cook time: 25 minutes

Ingredients:

- 4 pork chops (about 200 grams each)
- Salt and pepper, to taste
- 1 tablespoon olive oil
- 2 cloves garlic, minced
- 200 grams fresh spinach leaves
- 150 grams mozzarella cheese, sliced
- 1/2 teaspoon dried oregano
- 1/2 teaspoon dried basil

Directions:

1. Preheat the oven to 200°C (390°F).
2. Season the pork chops with salt and pepper on both sides.
3. Using a sharp knife, carefully cut a pocket into the side of each pork chop without cutting all the way through.
4. Heat the olive oil in a large ovenproof skillet over medium heat. Add the garlic and sauté until fragrant, about 1 minute. Add the spinach and cook until wilted, about 2-3 minutes. Remove from heat and let cool slightly.
5. Stuff each pork chop with the spinach mixture and mozzarella slices. Sprinkle the stuffed chops with oregano and basil.
6. In the same skillet, add the stuffed pork chops and sear for 2 minutes on each side until browned.
7. Transfer the skillet to the preheated oven and bake for 15 minutes, or until the pork chops are cooked through.
8. Serve hot and enjoy!

Nutritional Information: Estimated per serving: 360 calories, 38 grams protein, 2 grams carbohydrates, 22 grams fat, 1 gram fiber, 115 milligrams cholesterol, 350 milligrams sodium, 450 milligrams potassium.

Grilled Lamb Chops with Rosemary

Yield: 4 servings | Prep time: 5 minutes | Cook time: 10 minutes

Ingredients:

- 8 lamb chops (approximately 100 grams each)
- 2 tablespoons olive oil
- 2 tablespoons fresh rosemary leaves, chopped
- 4 cloves garlic, minced
- Salt and pepper, to taste
- 1 lemon, zested and juiced

Directions:

1. Preheat your grill to medium-high heat.
2. In a small bowl, mix together the olive oil, chopped rosemary, minced garlic, lemon zest, and lemon juice.
3. Season the lamb chops on both sides with salt and pepper.
4. Brush the rosemary mixture onto both sides of the lamb chops.
5. Place the lamb chops on the preheated grill and cook for 3-5 minutes per side, or until they reach your desired level of doneness.
6. Remove the lamb chops from the grill and let them rest for a few minutes before serving.
7. Serve the lamb chops with a side of your favorite low-carb vegetables and enjoy!

Nutritional Information: Estimated per serving: 290 calories, 24 grams protein, 1 gram carbohydrates, 21 grams fat, 0 grams fiber, 80 milligrams cholesterol, 90 milligrams sodium, 300 milligrams potassium.

Balsamic Glazed Chicken and Veggies

Yield: 4 servings | Prep time: 10 minutes | Cook time: 25 minutes

Ingredients:

- 4 chicken breasts (about 150 grams each)
- 2 tablespoons olive oil
- Salt and pepper, to taste
- 200 grams asparagus, trimmed
- 200 grams courgette (zucchini), sliced
- 200 grams cherry tomatoes, halved
- 1 red bell pepper, sliced
- 4 cloves garlic, minced
- 120 millilitres balsamic vinegar
- 1 teaspoon dried basil
- 1 teaspoon dried oregano

Directions:

1. Preheat your oven to 200°C (400°F).
2. Season chicken breasts with salt and pepper on both sides. Heat 1 tablespoon of olive oil in a large ovenproof skillet over medium-high heat. Add the chicken breasts and sear for 2-3 minutes on each side until browned. Remove chicken from the skillet and set aside.
3. In the same skillet, add the remaining 1 tablespoon of olive oil and add the asparagus, courgette, cherry tomatoes, and bell pepper. Sauté the vegetables for 2-3 minutes until slightly tender. Add the minced garlic and sauté for an additional 1 minute.
4. Place the seared chicken breasts on top of the vegetables. In a small bowl, combine the balsamic vinegar, dried basil, and dried oregano. Pour the mixture over the chicken and vegetables.
5. Transfer the skillet to the preheated oven and bake for 15-20 minutes, or until the chicken is cooked through and the vegetables are tender.
6. Remove from the oven and let it rest for a few minutes before serving.

Nutritional Information: Estimated per serving: 290 calories, 29 grams protein, 12 grams carbohydrates, 12 grams fat, 3 grams fiber, 70 milligrams cholesterol, 220 milligrams sodium, 550 milligrams potassium.

Thai Basil Beef Stir-fry

Yield: 4 servings | Prep time: 10 minutes | Cook time: 10 minutes

Ingredients:

- 500 grams beef steak, thinly sliced
- 2 tablespoons coconut oil
- 1 small red onion, sliced
- 3 cloves garlic, minced
- 1 red chilli, sliced (optional)
- 200 grams green beans, trimmed and cut into bite-sized pieces
- 200 grams broccoli, cut into small florets
- 2 tablespoons fish sauce
- 1 tablespoon soy sauce (or tamari for gluten-free)
- 1 teaspoon erythritol (or other keto-friendly sweetener)
- 1 handful fresh Thai basil leaves
- 1 lime, cut into wedges

Directions:

1. Heat 1 tablespoon of coconut oil in a large frying pan or wok over high heat. Add the beef slices and stir-fry for 2-3 minutes until browned. Remove from the pan and set aside.
2. In the same pan, add the remaining 1 tablespoon of coconut oil and reduce the heat to medium. Add the sliced onion, garlic, and chilli (if using). Stir-fry for 2 minutes until fragrant.
3. Add the green beans and broccoli to the pan. Stir-fry for another 2-3 minutes until the vegetables are slightly tender.
4. Return the beef to the pan and add the fish sauce, soy sauce, and erythritol. Stir well to coat the beef and vegetables in the sauce. Cook for another 2 minutes until heated through.
5. Remove from the heat and stir in the Thai basil leaves. Serve immediately with lime wedges on the side.

Nutritional Information: Estimated per serving: 280 calories, 28 grams protein, 8 grams carbohydrates, 15 grams fat, 3 grams fiber, 70 milligrams cholesterol, 780 milligrams sodium, 600 milligrams potassium.

Sausage and Cabbage Skillet

Yield: 4 servings | Prep time: 10 minutes | Cook time: 20 minutes

Ingredients:

- 500 grams sausage, sliced into rounds (choose a keto-friendly variety without added sugars or fillers)
- 1 tablespoon olive oil
- 1 small onion, chopped
- 3 cloves garlic, minced
- 1/2 head cabbage, shredded (about 500 grams)

- 1/4 teaspoon salt
- 1/4 teaspoon black pepper
- 1/2 teaspoon smoked paprika
- 1/4 teaspoon red pepper flakes (optional)
- 2 tablespoons apple cider vinegar
- 2 tablespoons fresh parsley, chopped

Directions:

1. Heat the olive oil in a large skillet over medium-high heat. Add the sliced sausage and cook for 4-5 minutes, turning occasionally, until browned on both sides. Remove the sausage from the skillet and set aside.
2. In the same skillet, add the chopped onion and minced garlic. Cook for 2-3 minutes until the onion is soft and translucent.
3. Add the shredded cabbage, salt, black pepper, smoked paprika, and red pepper flakes (if using) to the skillet. Stir well to combine. Cook for 5-7 minutes, stirring occasionally, until the cabbage is tender but still has some bite.
4. Return the sausage to the skillet and add the apple cider vinegar. Stir well to combine and heat through.
5. Remove from heat and sprinkle with chopped parsley. Serve immediately.

Nutritional Information: Estimated per serving: 400 calories, 18 grams protein, 10 grams carbohydrates, 33 grams fat, 4 grams fiber, 75 milligrams cholesterol, 980 milligrams sodium, 420 milligrams potassium.

Creamy Cajun Shrimp and Sausage Pasta

Yield: 4 servings | Prep time: 10 minutes | Cook time: 20 minutes

Ingredients:

- 300 grams large shrimp, peeled and deveined
- 200 grams keto-friendly sausage, sliced
- 2 tablespoons olive oil
- 1 small onion, chopped
- 3 cloves garlic, minced
- 2 teaspoons Cajun seasoning
- 1/2 teaspoon salt

- 1/4 teaspoon black pepper
- 1/4 teaspoon red pepper flakes (optional)
- 150 grams cherry tomatoes, halved
- 250 grams zucchini noodles (zoodles)
- 240 milliliters heavy cream
- 50 grams grated Parmesan cheese
- 2 tablespoons fresh parsley, chopped

Directions:

1. In a large skillet, heat the olive oil over medium-high heat. Add the sliced sausage and cook for 4-5 minutes, turning occasionally, until browned on both sides. Remove the sausage from the skillet and set aside.
2. In the same skillet, add the shrimp and cook for 2-3 minutes on each side until pink and opaque. Remove the shrimp from the skillet and set aside with the sausage.
3. Add the chopped onion and minced garlic to the skillet. Cook for 2-3 minutes until the onion is soft and translucent. Stir in the Cajun seasoning, salt, black pepper, and red pepper flakes (if using).
4. Add the cherry tomatoes and cook for 2-3 minutes until they start to soften. Stir in the zucchini noodles and cook for an additional 2-3 minutes until they are tender but still have some bite.
5. Pour in the heavy cream and bring to a simmer. Stir in the grated Parmesan cheese until melted and the sauce is creamy. Return the shrimp and sausage to the skillet and heat through.
6. Remove from heat and sprinkle with chopped parsley. Serve immediately.

Nutritional Information: Estimated per serving: 460 calories, 25 grams protein, 8 grams carbohydrates, 37 grams fat, 2 grams fiber, 190 milligrams cholesterol, 750 milligrams sodium, 420 milligrams potassium.

Eggplant Parmesan Casserole

Yield: 6 servings | Prep time: 15 minutes | Cook time: 45 minutes

Ingredients:

- 2 large eggplants (about 600 grams), sliced into 1 cm thick rounds
- 2 teaspoons salt
- 2 tablespoons olive oil
- 3 cloves garlic, minced
- 400 grams canned diced tomatoes
- 1 tablespoon tomato paste
- 1/2 teaspoon dried basil
- 1/2 teaspoon dried oregano
- 1/4 teaspoon black pepper
- 200 grams mozzarella cheese, shredded
- 50 grams grated Parmesan cheese
- 2 tablespoons fresh basil, chopped

Directions:

1. Preheat your oven to 190°C (375°F). Place the eggplant slices on a baking sheet lined with paper towels. Sprinkle both sides of the eggplant slices with salt and let them sit for 15 minutes to draw out moisture. Pat the eggplant slices dry with paper towels.
2. In a large skillet, heat the olive oil over medium heat. Add the garlic and cook for 1-2 minutes until fragrant. Stir in the diced tomatoes, tomato paste, dried basil, dried oregano, and black pepper. Bring to a simmer and cook for 5 minutes until the sauce thickens slightly. Remove from heat.
3. In a casserole dish, layer half of the eggplant slices, followed by half of the tomato sauce, half of the mozzarella cheese, and half of the Parmesan cheese. Repeat the layers with the remaining ingredients.
4. Cover the casserole with aluminum foil and bake for 25 minutes. Remove the foil and bake for an additional 20 minutes until the cheese is melted and bubbly. Remove from the oven and let it cool for a few minutes.
5. Sprinkle with fresh basil before serving.

Nutritional Information: Estimated per serving: 220 calories, 10 grams protein, 12 grams carbohydrates, 15 grams fat, 5 grams fiber, 30 milligrams cholesterol, 830 milligrams sodium, 520 milligrams potassium.

Beef and Broccoli Stir-fry

Yield: 4 servings | Prep time: 15 minutes | Cook time: 15 minutes

Ingredients:

- 400 grams beef sirloin, thinly sliced
- 4 cups broccoli florets (about 400 grams)
- 3 tablespoons coconut oil
- 3 cloves garlic, minced
- 1 small ginger root, minced (about 2 tablespoons)
- 60 milliliters soy sauce or tamari
- 60 milliliters beef broth
- 2 tablespoons sesame oil
- 1 tablespoon erythritol or another keto-friendly sweetener
- 1/4 teaspoon crushed red pepper flakes
- 1 tablespoon sesame seeds (optional)

Directions:

1. In a large wok or skillet, heat 2 tablespoons of coconut oil over medium-high heat. Add the beef slices and cook for 3-4 minutes until browned. Remove the beef from the skillet and set it aside.
2. In the same skillet, add the remaining coconut oil, garlic, and ginger. Cook for 1-2 minutes until fragrant. Add the broccoli florets and cook for 4-5 minutes until they begin to soften.
3. In a small bowl, whisk together the soy sauce, beef broth, sesame oil, erythritol, and red pepper flakes. Pour the sauce over the broccoli and add the cooked beef back into the skillet. Stir to combine and continue cooking for 2-3 minutes until everything is heated through.
4. Serve hot, optionally sprinkled with sesame seeds.

Nutritional Information: Estimated per serving: 375 calories, 29 grams protein, 8 grams carbohydrates, 26 grams fat, 3 grams fiber, 65 milligrams cholesterol, 970 milligrams sodium, 540 milligrams potassium.

Stuffed Bell Peppers with Ground Turkey

Yield: 4 servings | Prep time: 15 minutes | Cook time: 40 minutes

Ingredients:

- 4 large bell peppers (any colour), tops removed and seeds discarded
- 500 grams ground turkey
- 2 tablespoons olive oil
- 1 medium onion, chopped
- 3 cloves garlic, minced
- 200 grams canned diced tomatoes
- 1 teaspoon dried oregano
- 1 teaspoon dried basil
- 100 grams grated cheddar cheese
- Salt and pepper to taste
- Fresh parsley for garnish (optional)

Directions:

1. Preheat your oven to 190°C (375°F). In a large skillet, heat the olive oil over medium heat. Add the onions and garlic and sauté until softened, about 4-5 minutes.
2. Add the ground turkey to the skillet and cook until browned, breaking it up with a spatula, about 5-7 minutes. Stir in the diced tomatoes, dried oregano, dried basil, salt, and pepper. Cook for an additional 5 minutes until the flavors are combined.
3. Spoon the turkey mixture into the bell peppers, pressing down gently to fill the entire pepper. Place the stuffed peppers in a baking dish.
4. Sprinkle the grated cheddar cheese on top of the stuffed peppers. Cover the baking dish with aluminum foil.
5. Bake in the preheated oven for 30 minutes. Remove the foil and bake for an additional 10 minutes until the cheese is bubbly and golden brown.
6. Let the peppers cool for a few minutes before serving. Garnish with fresh parsley if desired.

Nutritional Information: Estimated per serving: 330 calories, 30 grams protein, 10 grams carbohydrates, 20 grams fat, 3 grams fiber, 90 milligrams cholesterol, 420 milligrams sodium, 600 milligrams potassium.

Lemon Herb Roasted Chicken

Yield: 4 servings | Prep time: 10 minutes | Cook time: 90 minutes

Ingredients:

- 1 whole chicken (about 1.5 kilograms)
- 2 lemons, zested and juiced
- 4 cloves garlic, minced
- 2 tablespoons fresh rosemary, chopped
- 2 tablespoons fresh thyme, chopped
- 4 tablespoons olive oil
- Salt and pepper to taste

Directions:

1. Preheat your oven to 190°C (375°F). In a small bowl, combine the lemon zest, lemon juice, garlic, rosemary, thyme, olive oil, salt, and pepper. Mix well to combine.
2. Pat the chicken dry with paper towels and season it generously with salt and pepper inside and out. Rub the herb mixture all over the chicken, ensuring that it gets under the skin as well.
3. Place the chicken on a rack in a roasting pan. Tie the legs together with kitchen twine and tuck the wing tips under the chicken.
4. Roast the chicken in the preheated oven for about 1 hour and 30 minutes, or until the internal temperature reaches 75°C (165°F). If the chicken starts to brown too much, you can cover it with aluminum foil.
5. Remove the chicken from the oven and let it rest for 10 minutes before carving and serving.

Nutritional Information: Estimated per serving: 480 calories, 40 grams protein, 4 grams carbohydrates, 35 grams fat, 1 gram fiber, 150 milligrams cholesterol, 200 milligrams sodium, 450 milligrams potassium.

Zucchini Lasagna with Beef and Ricotta

Yield: 6 servings | Prep time: 20 minutes | Cook time: 60 minutes

Ingredients:

- 4 large zucchinis (about 800 grams), thinly sliced lengthwise
- 500 grams ground beef
- 2 tablespoons olive oil
- 1 medium onion, finely chopped
- 3 cloves garlic, minced
- 400 grams canned crushed tomatoes
- 2 teaspoons dried oregano
- 2 teaspoons dried basil
- 250 grams ricotta cheese
- 200 grams grated mozzarella cheese
- 50 grams grated Parmesan cheese
- 1 large egg
- Salt and pepper to taste
- Fresh basil leaves for garnish (optional)

Directions:

1. Preheat your oven to 190°C (375°F). In a large skillet, heat the olive oil over medium heat. Add the onions and garlic and cook until they are soft, about 3-4 minutes. Add the ground beef, breaking it up with a spatula, and cook until browned, about 7-8 minutes.
2. Stir in the crushed tomatoes, dried oregano, dried basil, salt, and pepper. Bring the mixture to a simmer and let it cook for about 10 minutes until the flavors meld together. Remove from heat and set aside.
3. In a medium bowl, combine the ricotta cheese, egg, and half of the grated Parmesan cheese. Season with salt and pepper and mix until well combined.
4. In a 9x13 inch baking dish, layer the sliced zucchini, followed by the beef and tomato sauce, then the ricotta mixture, and finally a layer of mozzarella cheese. Repeat the layers until all the ingredients are used up, finishing with a layer of mozzarella cheese on top.
5. Sprinkle the remaining Parmesan cheese on top and cover the baking dish with aluminum foil. Bake in the preheated oven for 40 minutes. Remove the foil and bake for an additional 10-15 minutes until the cheese is bubbly and golden brown.
6. Let the lasagna rest for about 10 minutes before slicing and serving. Garnish with fresh basil leaves if desired.

Nutritional Information: Estimated per serving: 480 calories, 32 grams protein, 12 grams carbohydrates, 34 grams fat, 3 grams fiber, 120 milligrams cholesterol, 790 milligrams sodium, 740 milligrams potassium.

Keto-Friendly Fish and Seafood Dishes

Garlic Butter Shrimp Scampi
Yield: 4 servings | Prep time: 10 minutes | Cook time: 10 minutes

Ingredients:

- 450 grams large shrimp, peeled and deveined
- 120 grams butter
- 6 cloves garlic, minced
- 60 milliliters dry white wine (optional)
- 2 tablespoons fresh lemon juice
- 2 tablespoons fresh parsley, chopped
- Salt and pepper to taste
- 2 tablespoons olive oil
- Crushed red pepper flakes (optional)

Directions:

1. In a large skillet, heat olive oil over medium heat. Add the shrimp and cook until they begin to turn pink, about 2-3 minutes per side. Remove the shrimp and set them aside.
2. In the same skillet, add the butter and garlic. Sauté the garlic until it's fragrant, about 1 minute.
3. If using wine, add it to the skillet and bring it to a simmer. Let it simmer for about 2 minutes, allowing the wine to reduce.
4. Add the lemon juice, parsley, and cooked shrimp back to the skillet. Season with salt, pepper, and crushed red pepper flakes if using. Toss everything together to coat the shrimp in the sauce.
5. Serve the shrimp scampi immediately, garnished with additional parsley if desired.

Nutritional Information: Estimated per serving: 320 calories, 25 grams protein, 2 grams carbohydrates, 23 grams fat, 0 grams fiber, 180 milligrams cholesterol, 450 milligrams sodium, 150 milligrams potassium.

Grilled Swordfish Steaks with Salsa Verde
Yield: 4 servings | Prep time: 15 minutes | Cook time: 10 minutes

Ingredients:

- 4 swordfish steaks (about 150 grams each)
- Salt and pepper to taste
- 2 tablespoons olive oil

For the Salsa Verde:
- 60 milliliters extra-virgin olive oil
- 30 milliliters red wine vinegar
- 2 cloves garlic, minced
- 1 small shallot, finely chopped
- 20 grams fresh parsley, chopped
- 10 grams fresh basil, chopped
- 10 grams fresh mint, chopped
- 2 teaspoons capers, drained and chopped
- 1 teaspoon Dijon mustard
- Zest and juice of 1 lemon
- Salt and pepper to taste

Directions:

1. Preheat your grill to medium-high heat. Season the swordfish steaks with salt and pepper, and brush them with olive oil.
2. Grill the swordfish steaks for about 4-5 minutes per side or until they are cooked through and have nice grill marks.
3. While the swordfish is grilling, make the salsa verde. In a bowl, combine the olive oil, red wine vinegar, garlic, shallot, parsley, basil, mint, capers, mustard, lemon zest, and lemon juice. Season with salt and pepper to taste, and mix well.
4. Once the swordfish steaks are done grilling, remove them from the grill and let them rest for a few minutes.
5. Serve the swordfish steaks with a generous spoonful of salsa verde on top.

Nutritional Information: Estimated per serving: 370 calories, 29 grams protein, 3 grams carbohydrates, 27 grams fat, 1 grams fiber, 60 milligrams cholesterol, 320 milligrams sodium, 480 milligrams potassium.

Lemon-Dill Baked Salmon

Yield: 4 servings | Prep time: 10 minutes | Cook time: 15 minutes

Ingredients:

- 4 salmon fillets (about 150 grams each)
- Salt and pepper to taste
- 2 tablespoons olive oil
- 2 tablespoons fresh dill, chopped
- 1 lemon, zested and juiced
- 2 cloves garlic, minced

Directions:

1. Preheat your oven to 200°C (390°F). Line a baking tray with parchment paper.
2. Season the salmon fillets with salt and pepper, and place them skin-side down on the prepared baking tray.
3. In a small bowl, combine the olive oil, dill, lemon zest, lemon juice, and minced garlic. Mix well.
4. Spoon the lemon-dill mixture over the salmon fillets, making sure to cover each fillet evenly.
5. Bake the salmon in the preheated oven for about 12-15 minutes or until the salmon is cooked through and flakes easily with a fork.
6. Remove the salmon from the oven and let it rest for a few minutes before serving.

Nutritional Information: Estimated per serving: 260 calories, 24 grams protein, 1 gram carbohydrates, 17 grams fat, 0 grams fiber, 65 milligrams cholesterol, 190 milligrams sodium, 580 milligrams potassium.

Crab Stuffed Avocado

Yield: 4 servings | Prep time: 15 minutes | Cook time: 0 minutes

Ingredients:

- 2 large avocados, halved and pitted
- 200 grams crab meat, drained
- 4 tablespoons mayonnaise
- 1 tablespoon fresh lemon juice
- 1 tablespoon fresh parsley, chopped
- 2 teaspoons Dijon mustard
- 1/2 small red onion, finely diced
- Salt and pepper to taste
- Fresh chives, for garnish

Directions:

1. In a mixing bowl, combine crab meat, mayonnaise, lemon juice, parsley, Dijon mustard, red onion, salt, and pepper. Mix well to combine.
2. Carefully scoop out some of the avocado flesh, leaving a 1 cm thick border around the edges. Dice the scooped-out avocado and gently fold it into the crab mixture.
3. Spoon the crab mixture into the avocado halves, mounding it on top.
4. Garnish with fresh chives.
5. Serve immediately, or refrigerate for up to 2 hours before serving.

Nutritional Information: Estimated per serving: 290 calories, 11 grams protein, 8 grams carbohydrates, 25 grams fat, 6 grams fiber, 50 milligrams cholesterol, 290 milligrams sodium, 580 milligrams potassium.

Grilled Tuna Steaks with Chimichurri

Yield: 4 servings | Prep time: 20 minutes | Cook time: 10 minutes

Ingredients:

- 4 tuna steaks (about 150 grams each)
- 2 tablespoons olive oil
- Salt and pepper, to season

For the Chimichurri:
- 60 ml olive oil
- 2 tablespoons red wine vinegar

- 1 bunch fresh parsley, finely chopped
- 4 cloves garlic, minced
- 2 small red chillies, deseeded and finely chopped (adjust based on heat preference)
- 1/2 teaspoon salt
- 1/4 teaspoon black pepper
- 1/4 teaspoon dried oregano

Directions:

1. Preheat grill to high heat. While it's heating, brush both sides of the tuna steaks with olive oil and season with salt and pepper.
2. For the chimichurri, combine all ingredients in a bowl and mix well. Set aside for the flavours to meld.
3. Place tuna steaks on the grill and cook for about 2-3 minutes on each side for medium-rare, or until desired doneness.
4. Remove tuna steaks from the grill and let them rest for a few minutes. Serve with a generous amount of chimichurri on top.

Nutritional Information: Estimated per serving: 340 calories, 35 grams protein, 1 gram carbohydrates, 22 grams fat, 0.2 grams fiber, 45 milligrams cholesterol, 330 milligrams sodium, 500 milligrams potassium.

Keto Lobster Bisque

Yield: 4 servings | Prep time: 10 minutes | Cook time: 35 minutes

Ingredients:

- 450 grams cooked lobster meat, cut into chunks
- 60 grams butter
- 1 small onion, finely chopped (about 70 grams)
- 2 cloves garlic, minced
- 1 teaspoon paprika
- 1/2 teaspoon cayenne pepper

- 1/4 teaspoon white pepper
- 240 ml chicken or seafood broth
- 240 ml heavy cream
- 2 tablespoons tomato paste
- 1 bay leaf
- 1 tablespoon fresh tarragon, chopped
- Salt, to taste

Directions:

1. In a large pot over medium heat, melt butter. Add onions and garlic, sautéing until the onions are translucent, about 5 minutes.
2. Stir in the paprika, cayenne pepper, and white pepper. Cook for 1 minute until the spices are fragrant.
3. Add the tomato paste and cook, stirring constantly, for 1-2 minutes until the tomato paste darkens in color.
4. Add the chicken or seafood broth, heavy cream, bay leaf, and tarragon. Bring to a simmer and cook for 15 minutes, stirring occasionally.
5. Remove the bay leaf and use an immersion blender to puree the soup until smooth. Alternatively, you can transfer the soup to a blender and blend in batches.
6. Add the lobster meat to the pot and simmer for an additional 5 minutes until the lobster is heated through. Season with salt to taste.
7. Serve hot, garnished with additional tarragon if desired.

Nutritional Information: Estimated per serving: 385 calories, 21 grams protein, 5 grams carbohydrates, 32 grams fat, 1 gram fiber, 135 milligrams cholesterol, 550 milligrams sodium, 250 milligrams potassium.

Spicy Tuna Avocado Boats

Yield: 4 servings | Prep time: 10 minutes | Cook time: 0 minutes

Ingredients:

- 2 ripe avocados, halved and pitted
- 200 grams canned tuna, drained
- 60 grams mayonnaise
- 1 tablespoon Sriracha sauce
- 1 tablespoon lime juice
- 1 tablespoon chopped fresh coriander
- 1 small red chilli, finely chopped (optional)
- Salt and pepper, to taste
- Extra coriander leaves, for garnish

Directions:

1. In a medium bowl, mix together the tuna, mayonnaise, Sriracha sauce, lime juice, chopped coriander, and chopped chilli (if using). Season with salt and pepper to taste.
2. Spoon the tuna mixture evenly into the avocado halves.
3. Garnish with extra coriander leaves.
4. Serve immediately as a light meal or appetizer.

Nutritional Information: Estimated per serving: 238 calories, 12 grams protein, 9 grams carbohydrates, 19 grams fat, 7 grams fiber, 18 milligrams cholesterol, 320 milligrams sodium, 470 milligrams potassium.

Seared Scallops with Brown Butter Sauce

Yield: 4 servings | Prep time: 5 minutes | Cook time: 10 minutes

Ingredients:

- 12 large scallops (about 500 grams)
- Salt and pepper, to taste
- 2 tablespoons olive oil
- 60 grams unsalted butter
- 1 tablespoon lemon juice
- 1 tablespoon chopped fresh parsley
- 2 cloves garlic, minced

Directions:

1. Pat the scallops dry with paper towels and season both sides with salt and pepper.
2. In a large skillet, heat the olive oil over medium-high heat until hot. Add the scallops to the skillet and sear for about 2 minutes on each side, until they are golden brown and cooked through. Remove the scallops from the skillet and set them aside.
3. In the same skillet, add the butter and cook over medium heat until it turns a golden brown colour, about 3 minutes. Add the garlic and sauté for about 1 minute, until fragrant.
4. Remove the skillet from the heat and stir in the lemon juice and parsley. Season with salt and pepper to taste.
5. Spoon the brown butter sauce over the scallops and serve immediately.

Nutritional Information: Estimated per serving: 270 calories, 19 grams protein, 2 grams carbohydrates, 20 grams fat, 0 grams fiber, 75 milligrams cholesterol, 280 milligrams sodium, 250 milligrams potassium.

Lemon-Parsley Baked Cod

Yield: 4 servings | Prep time: 10 minutes | Cook time: 15 minutes

Ingredients:

- 4 cod fillets (about 600 grams total)
- 2 tablespoons olive oil
- 1 teaspoon lemon zest
- 2 tablespoons fresh lemon juice
- 2 cloves garlic, minced
- 2 tablespoons chopped fresh parsley
- Salt and pepper, to taste
- 1 tablespoon unsalted butter, cut into small pieces

Directions:

1. Preheat your oven to 200°C (390°F). Grease a baking dish with olive oil or non-stick spray.
2. In a small bowl, mix together the olive oil, lemon zest, lemon juice, garlic, parsley, salt, and pepper.
3. Place the cod fillets in the prepared baking dish and pour the lemon-parsley mixture over the top. Dot the tops of the fillets with the small pieces of butter.
4. Bake the cod in the preheated oven for about 15 minutes, or until the fish flakes easily with a fork.
5. Serve the baked cod with the sauce from the baking dish spooned over the top.

Nutritional Information: Estimated per serving: 210 calories, 25 grams protein, 1 gram carbohydrates, 12 grams fat, 0 grams fiber, 60 milligrams cholesterol, 105 milligrams sodium, 380 milligrams potassium.

Cilantro Lime Shrimp with Zucchini Noodles

Yield: 4 servings | Prep time: 15 minutes | Cook time: 10 minutes

Ingredients:

- 450 grams large raw shrimp, peeled and deveined
- 4 medium zucchini (about 800 grams), spiralized into noodles
- 2 tablespoons olive oil
- 4 cloves garlic, minced
- 1/4 teaspoon red pepper flakes (optional)
- 1/4 cup fresh lime juice
- 1/4 cup chopped fresh cilantro
- Salt and pepper, to taste

Directions:

1. In a large skillet, heat the olive oil over medium heat. Add the garlic and red pepper flakes (if using) and sauté for about 1 minute, or until fragrant.
2. Add the shrimp to the skillet and cook for 2-3 minutes on each side, or until pink and cooked through.
3. Remove the shrimp from the skillet and set aside. Add the zucchini noodles to the skillet and cook for 2-3 minutes, or until just tender. Season with salt and pepper.
4. Return the shrimp to the skillet and add the lime juice and cilantro. Toss to combine and heat for an additional 1-2 minutes.
5. Serve the shrimp and zucchini noodles hot, with additional cilantro and lime wedges, if desired.

Nutritional Information: Estimated per serving: 210 calories, 24 grams protein, 10 grams carbohydrates, 9 grams fat, 3 grams fiber, 180 milligrams cholesterol, 350 milligrams sodium, 750 milligrams potassium.

Creamy Clam Chowder

Yield: 6 servings | Prep time: 20 minutes | Cook time: 30 minutes

Ingredients:

- 150 grams diced bacon
- 1 medium onion, finely chopped (about 150 grams)
- 2 cloves garlic, minced
- 1 celery stalk, finely chopped (about 50 grams)
- 1 small cauliflower, cut into small florets (about 400 grams)
- 400 grams clams, chopped, with juice reserved
- 500 ml chicken or vegetable broth
- 250 ml heavy cream
- 1 teaspoon fresh thyme leaves, chopped
- Salt and pepper, to taste
- Fresh parsley, chopped, for garnish

Directions:

1. In a large pot or Dutch oven, cook the bacon over medium heat until crisp. Remove the bacon from the pot and set aside, leaving the bacon grease in the pot.
2. Add the onion, garlic, and celery to the pot and sauté in the bacon grease until the vegetables are softened, about 5 minutes.
3. Add the cauliflower florets to the pot, along with the reserved clam juice and chicken or vegetable broth. Bring to a simmer and cook until the cauliflower is tender, about 10 minutes.
4. Add the chopped clams, heavy cream, and thyme to the pot. Continue to simmer for an additional 5 minutes, until the clams are heated through. Season with salt and pepper to taste.
5. Serve the chowder hot, topped with the reserved bacon and garnished with fresh parsley.

Nutritional Information: Estimated per serving: 320 calories, 18 grams protein, 8 grams carbohydrates, 26 grams fat, 2 grams fiber, 90 milligrams cholesterol, 850 milligrams sodium, 500 milligrams potassium.

Grilled Sardines with Garlic and Lemon

Yield: 4 servings | Prep time: 15 minutes | Cook time: 6 minutes

Ingredients:

- 8 fresh sardines, cleaned and gutted (about 600 grams)
- 4 cloves garlic, minced
- Zest and juice of 2 lemons
- 60 ml olive oil
- Salt and pepper, to taste
- Fresh parsley, chopped, for garnish

Directions:

1. Preheat the grill to high heat. In a small bowl, mix together the minced garlic, lemon zest, lemon juice, and olive oil. Season with salt and pepper to taste.
2. Brush the sardines on both sides with the garlic and lemon mixture, making sure to get some inside the cavity of each fish.
3. Grill the sardines for 2-3 minutes on each side, until the skin is charred and the fish is cooked through.
4. Remove the sardines from the grill and transfer them to a serving platter. Drizzle any remaining garlic and lemon mixture over the top.
5. Garnish with chopped parsley and serve immediately.

Nutritional Information: Estimated per serving: 240 calories, 24 grams protein, 3 grams carbohydrates, 15 grams fat, 0 grams fiber, 90 milligrams cholesterol, 180 milligrams sodium, 370 milligrams potassium.

Keto Seafood Gumbo

Yield: 4 servings | Prep time: 15 minutes | Cook time: 45 minutes

Ingredients:

- 300 grams raw shrimp, peeled and deveined
- 150 grams white fish fillet, cubed
- 150 grams crab meat
- 4 cups chicken stock (about 1 litre)
- 2 tablespoons olive oil (30 ml)
- 1 large onion, chopped
- 2 celery stalks, chopped
- 1 bell pepper, chopped
- 4 cloves garlic, minced
- 1 teaspoon smoked paprika
- 1 teaspoon ground thyme
- 1/2 teaspoon cayenne pepper
- 1/2 teaspoon black pepper
- 1 bay leaf
- 200 grams chopped tomatoes
- 150 grams okra, sliced
- Salt to taste
- Fresh parsley, chopped, for garnish
- Green onions, sliced, for garnish

Directions:

1. In a large pot or Dutch oven, heat the olive oil over medium heat. Add the onion, celery, and bell pepper, and cook until softened, about 5 minutes. Stir in the garlic and cook for another minute.
2. Add the smoked paprika, thyme, cayenne pepper, black pepper, and bay leaf. Stir to coat the vegetables with the spices.
3. Add the chicken stock, chopped tomatoes, and okra. Bring the mixture to a simmer and cook for 30 minutes.
4. Add the shrimp, fish, and crab meat to the pot. Cook until the seafood is opaque and cooked through, about 5 minutes. Season with salt to taste.
5. Remove the bay leaf and serve the gumbo hot, garnished with chopped parsley and sliced green onions.

Nutritional Information: Estimated per serving: 240 calories, 28 grams protein, 10 grams carbohydrates, 10 grams fat, 2 grams fiber, 160 milligrams cholesterol, 640 milligrams sodium, 570 milligrams potassium.

Baked Trout with Almond Pesto

Yield: 4 servings | Prep time: 10 minutes | Cook time: 20 minutes

Ingredients:

- 4 trout fillets (approximately 600 grams total)
- 100 grams almonds
- 50 grams fresh basil leaves
- 2 cloves garlic
- 60 ml olive oil
- 50 grams grated Parmesan cheese
- Salt and black pepper, to taste
- 1 tablespoon lemon juice (15 ml)
- 1 teaspoon lemon zest

Directions:

1. Preheat your oven to 200°C (392°F).
2. In a food processor, add the almonds, basil, garlic, olive oil, Parmesan cheese, lemon juice, and zest. Process until a paste forms. Season with salt and pepper to taste.
3. Arrange the trout fillets on a baking sheet lined with parchment paper. Season each fillet with salt and black pepper.
4. Spread the almond pesto over each trout fillet.
5. Bake in the preheated oven for 12-15 minutes, or until the trout is opaque and flakes easily with a fork.
6. Serve hot, and enjoy!

Nutritional Information: Estimated per serving: 450 calories, 42 grams protein, 4 grams carbohydrates, 30 grams fat, 2 grams fiber, 95 milligrams cholesterol, 250 milligrams sodium, 660 milligrams potassium.

Sared Mackerel with Green Beans

Yield: 4 servings | Prep time: 10 minutes | Cook time: 15 minutes

Ingredients:

- 4 mackerel fillets (approximately 600 grams total)
- 300 grams green beans, trimmed
- 2 tablespoons olive oil (30 ml)
- Salt and black pepper, to taste

- 1 tablespoon lemon juice (15 ml)
- 1 teaspoon lemon zest
- 2 cloves garlic, minced
- 1 teaspoon fresh thyme leaves
- 1 tablespoon butter (15 grams)

Directions:

1. Season the mackerel fillets with salt, black pepper, and lemon zest. Set aside.
2. In a large skillet, heat 1 tablespoon of olive oil over medium-high heat. Add the green beans, season with salt and black pepper, and sauté for 5-7 minutes, or until they are tender-crisp. Remove from the skillet and set aside.
3. In the same skillet, add the remaining tablespoon of olive oil and increase the heat to high. Once hot, add the mackerel fillets, skin-side down, and sear for 2-3 minutes, or until the skin is crispy. Flip the fillets and sear for an additional 2 minutes.
4. Lower the heat to medium, add the minced garlic, thyme, and butter. Continue to cook for 2-3 more minutes, basting the fillets with the buttery sauce.
5. Return the green beans to the skillet, toss with the buttery sauce, and cook for 1 more minute.
6. Serve the mackerel fillets with the green beans, drizzle with lemon juice, and enjoy!

Nutritional Information: Estimated per serving: 310 calories, 30 grams protein, 5 grams carbohydrates, 20 grams fat, 2 grams fiber, 85 milligrams cholesterol, 220 milligrams sodium, 600 milligrams potassium.

Delicious Keto Meat and Poultry Recipes

Balsamic Glazed Pork Chops

Yield: 4 servings | Prep time: 5 minutes | Cook time: 20 minutes

Ingredients:

- 4 boneless pork chops (approximately 600 grams total)
- Salt and black pepper, to taste
- 2 tablespoons olive oil (30 ml)
- 4 cloves garlic, minced
- 60 ml balsamic vinegar
- 2 tablespoons Dijon mustard (30 grams)
- 1 tablespoon erythritol (15 grams)
- 1 teaspoon fresh rosemary, chopped
- 1 teaspoon fresh thyme, chopped

Directions:

1. Season the pork chops on both sides with salt and black pepper.
2. In a large skillet, heat the olive oil over medium-high heat. Once hot, add the pork chops and cook for 5-7 minutes on each side, or until they are browned and cooked through. Remove the pork chops from the skillet and set aside.
3. In the same skillet, add the minced garlic and cook for 1 minute, or until fragrant. Add the balsamic vinegar, Dijon mustard, erythritol, rosemary, and thyme. Stir to combine and bring to a simmer. Cook for 3-5 minutes, or until the sauce has thickened.
4. Return the pork chops to the skillet and spoon the balsamic glaze over the top. Cook for an additional 1-2 minutes, or until the pork chops are heated through.
5. Serve the pork chops with the balsamic glaze and enjoy!

Nutritional Information: Estimated per serving: 330 calories, 35 grams protein, 5 grams carbohydrates, 18 grams fat, 0 grams fiber, 90 milligrams cholesterol, 310 milligrams sodium, 400 milligrams potassium.

Garlic Herb Lamb Chops

Yield: 4 servings | Prep time: 10 minutes | Cook time: 10 minutes

Ingredients:

- 8 lamb chops (approximately 800 grams total)
- 2 tablespoons olive oil (30 ml)
- 4 cloves garlic, minced
- 1 tablespoon rosemary, chopped (15 grams)
- 1 tablespoon thyme, chopped (15 grams)
- 1 tablespoon parsley, chopped (15 grams)
- Salt and black pepper, to taste
- Zest of 1 lemon
- Juice of 1 lemon (approximately 30 ml)

Directions:

1. In a small bowl, mix together the olive oil, garlic, rosemary, thyme, parsley, salt, black pepper, lemon zest, and lemon juice to create the herb mixture.
2. Season the lamb chops with salt and black pepper on both sides. Then, rub the herb mixture onto both sides of the lamb chops, making sure to coat them evenly.
3. Preheat a grill or grilling pan over medium-high heat. Once hot, place the lamb chops onto the grill or grilling pan and cook for 4-5 minutes on each side, or until they reach your desired level of doneness.
4. Once cooked, remove the lamb chops from the grill or grilling pan and let them rest for a few minutes before serving.

Nutritional Information: Estimated per serving: 450 calories, 38 grams protein, 2 grams carbohydrates, 32 grams fat, 0.5 grams fiber, 115 milligrams cholesterol, 220 milligrams sodium, 410 milligrams potassium.

Chicken Tikka Masala

Yield: 4 servings | Prep time: 15 minutes | Cook time: 35 minutes

Ingredients:

- 600 grams chicken breast, cubed
- 2 tablespoons olive oil (30 ml)
- 1 onion, finely chopped (approx. 150 grams)
- 4 cloves garlic, minced
- 1 tablespoon ginger, minced (15 grams)
- 2 tablespoons tomato paste (30 grams)
- 1 tablespoon garam masala (15 grams)
- 1 teaspoon turmeric (5 grams)
- 1 teaspoon cumin (5 grams)
- 1 teaspoon paprika (5 grams)
- 1 teaspoon chili powder (5 grams)
- 1/2 teaspoon cinnamon (2.5 grams)
- 1/2 teaspoon cayenne pepper (2.5 grams)
- Salt and black pepper, to taste
- 400 ml canned tomatoes, crushed
- 250 ml heavy cream
- 1 tablespoon fresh cilantro, chopped (optional)

Directions:

1. Heat the olive oil in a large skillet over medium-high heat. Add the chicken cubes and cook until browned on all sides, about 5 minutes. Remove the chicken from the skillet and set aside.
2. In the same skillet, add the onion and cook until softened, about 5 minutes. Add the garlic and ginger and cook for another 1 minute until fragrant.
3. Add the tomato paste, garam masala, turmeric, cumin, paprika, chili powder, cinnamon, cayenne pepper, salt, and black pepper. Stir well to combine.
4. Add the crushed tomatoes and bring to a simmer. Add the chicken back into the skillet and reduce heat to low. Cover and cook for 25 minutes, stirring occasionally.
5. Stir in the heavy cream and continue cooking for another 5 minutes. Season to taste with salt and black pepper.
6. Garnish with fresh cilantro, if desired, and serve.

Nutritional Information: Estimated per serving: 470 calories, 36 grams protein, 11 grams carbohydrates, 31 grams fat, 3 grams fiber, 150 milligrams cholesterol, 480 milligrams sodium, 760 milligrams potassium.

Rosemary Roasted Turkey Breast

Yield: 6 servings | Prep time: 10 minutes | Cook time: 60 minutes

Ingredients:

- 1 turkey breast, bone-in, skin-on (approximately 1.5 kilograms)
- 2 tablespoons olive oil (30 ml)
- 2 tablespoons fresh rosemary, finely chopped (30 grams)
- 4 cloves garlic, minced
- 1 teaspoon salt (5 grams)
- 1/2 teaspoon black pepper (2.5 grams)
- 1/2 teaspoon paprika (2.5 grams)
- 1/2 teaspoon onion powder (2.5 grams)
- 1/2 teaspoon dried thyme (2.5 grams)

Directions:

1. Preheat the oven to 190°C (375°F).
2. In a small bowl, combine the olive oil, rosemary, garlic, salt, black pepper, paprika, onion powder, and dried thyme to create a paste.
3. Rinse the turkey breast and pat it dry with paper towels. Gently loosen the skin from the meat with your fingers, being careful not to tear it. Rub the herb paste under the skin, spreading it evenly over the meat.
4. Place the turkey breast on a rack in a roasting pan, skin side up. Roast in the preheated oven for about 60 minutes, or until the internal temperature reaches 74°C (165°F) and the skin is golden brown.
5. Remove the turkey from the oven and let it rest for 10 minutes before carving. Slice and serve.

Nutritional Information: Estimated per serving: 295 calories, 49 grams protein, 1 gram carbohydrates, 11 grams fat, 0 grams fiber, 130 milligrams cholesterol, 510 milligrams sodium, 420 milligrams potassium.

Keto Beef Stroganoff
Yield: 4 servings | Prep time: 15 minutes | Cook time: 20 minutes

Ingredients:

- 500 grams beef sirloin steak, sliced thinly
- 1 large onion, finely chopped (approximately 150 grams)
- 200 grams mushrooms, sliced
- 2 cloves garlic, minced
- 1 tablespoon olive oil (15 ml)
- 200 ml beef broth
- 100 ml heavy cream
- 1 tablespoon Dijon mustard (15 grams)
- 1 tablespoon Worcestershire sauce (15 ml)
- 1 teaspoon paprika (5 grams)
- Salt and black pepper, to taste
- 2 tablespoons fresh parsley, chopped (30 grams)
- 200 grams cauliflower rice, for serving

Directions:

1. In a large frying pan, heat the olive oil over medium heat. Add the sliced beef to the pan and sear on both sides until browned but not fully cooked through. Remove the beef from the pan and set it aside.
2. In the same pan, add the onion, mushrooms, and garlic, and sauté until the vegetables are softened, about 5 minutes.
3. Stir in the beef broth, heavy cream, Dijon mustard, Worcestershire sauce, paprika, salt, and black pepper. Bring the mixture to a simmer, then return the beef to the pan.
4. Continue to simmer the mixture until the beef is cooked through and the sauce has thickened, about 10 minutes.
5. Serve the beef stroganoff over cauliflower rice and garnish with fresh parsley.

Nutritional Information: Estimated per serving: 365 calories, 28 grams protein, 10 grams carbohydrates, 24 grams fat, 3 grams fiber, 90 milligrams cholesterol, 520 milligrams sodium, 750 milligrams potassium.

Lemon-Thyme Roasted Chicken
Yield: 4 servings | Prep time: 10 minutes | Cook time: 90 minutes

Ingredients:

- 1 whole chicken (about 1.8 kilograms)
- 2 tablespoons olive oil (30 ml)
- 2 lemons, zested and juiced
- 2 tablespoons fresh thyme leaves (30 grams)
- 4 cloves garlic, minced
- 1 teaspoon salt (5 grams)
- 1/2 teaspoon black pepper (2.5 grams)

Directions:

1. Preheat the oven to 190°C (375°F).
2. In a small bowl, combine the olive oil, lemon zest, lemon juice, thyme, garlic, salt, and black pepper to create a marinade.
3. Rinse the chicken and pat it dry with paper towels. Place the chicken on a rack in a roasting pan and rub the marinade all over the chicken, both inside the cavity and on the outside.
4. Roast the chicken in the preheated oven for approximately 90 minutes, or until the internal temperature reaches 74°C (165°F) and the skin is golden brown and crispy.
5. Remove the chicken from the oven and let it rest for 10 minutes before carving. Slice and serve.

Nutritional Information: Estimated per serving: 500 calories, 40 grams protein, 4 grams carbohydrates, 36 grams fat, 1 gram fiber, 170 milligrams cholesterol, 680 milligrams sodium, 450 milligrams potassium.

Bacon-Wrapped Filet Mignon

Yield: 4 servings | Prep time: 10 minutes | Cook time: 15 minutes

Ingredients:

- 4 filet mignon steaks, each about 170 grams
- 8 slices of bacon (about 200 grams)
- 2 tablespoons olive oil (30 ml)
- 1 teaspoon salt (5 grams)
- 1/2 teaspoon black pepper (2.5 grams)
- 4 sprigs of fresh rosemary

Directions:

1. Preheat your oven to 220°C (425°F).
2. Season each filet mignon steak with salt and pepper. Wrap two slices of bacon around each steak and secure with toothpicks. Place a sprig of rosemary on top of each steak.
3. In a large oven-safe skillet, heat the olive oil over medium-high heat. Once the oil is hot, add the steaks to the pan and sear on all sides until the bacon is crispy, about 2 minutes per side.
4. Transfer the skillet to the preheated oven and roast for 7-10 minutes, depending on your desired level of doneness (7 minutes for medium-rare, 10 minutes for medium).
5. Remove the skillet from the oven and let the steaks rest for 5 minutes before removing the toothpicks and serving.

Nutritional Information: Estimated per serving: 480 calories, 30 grams protein, 1 gram carbohydrates, 38 grams fat, 0 grams fiber, 100 milligrams cholesterol, 1100 milligrams sodium, 300 milligrams potassium.

Creamy Tuscan Garlic Chicken

Yield: 4 servings | Prep time: 10 minutes | Cook time: 20 minutes

Ingredients:

- 4 boneless, skinless chicken breasts (about 600 grams)
- 1 teaspoon salt (5 grams)
- 1/2 teaspoon black pepper (2.5 grams)
- 2 tablespoons olive oil (30 ml)
- 5 cloves garlic, minced (about 15 grams)
- 1 cup heavy cream (240 ml)
- 1/2 cup chicken broth (120 ml)
- 1 teaspoon Italian seasoning (1 gram)
- 1/2 cup grated Parmesan cheese (50 grams)
- 1 cup spinach leaves (30 grams)
- 1/2 cup sun-dried tomatoes (55 grams)

Directions:

1. Season the chicken breasts with salt and pepper. In a large skillet, heat the olive oil over medium-high heat. Add the chicken breasts and cook for about 4-5 minutes on each side, until golden brown. Remove the chicken and set aside.
2. In the same skillet, add the minced garlic and sauté for about 1 minute, until fragrant. Add the heavy cream, chicken broth, Italian seasoning, and Parmesan cheese. Stir to combine and bring to a simmer.
3. Add the spinach leaves and sun-dried tomatoes to the skillet. Cook for 2-3 minutes, until the spinach has wilted.
4. Return the chicken to the skillet and cook for an additional 3-4 minutes, until the chicken is cooked through and the sauce has thickened.
5. Serve the chicken with the creamy sauce on top.

Nutritional Information: Estimated per serving: 470 calories, 32 grams protein, 8 grams carbohydrates, 35 grams fat, 2 grams fiber, 145 milligrams cholesterol, 800 milligrams sodium, 400 milligrams potassium.

Grilled Moroccan Lamb Kebabs

Yield: 4 servings | Prep time: 20 minutes | Cook time: 10 minutes

Ingredients:

- 600 grams of lamb leg or shoulder, cut into 2 cm cubes
- 4 garlic cloves, minced (about 12 grams)
- 1 tablespoon ground cumin (6 grams)
- 1 tablespoon ground paprika (6 grams)
- 1 teaspoon ground turmeric (2 grams)
- 1 teaspoon ground coriander (2 grams)
- 1 teaspoon ground cinnamon (2 grams)
- 1 teaspoon chili powder (2 grams)
- 1 teaspoon salt (5 grams)
- 1/2 teaspoon black pepper (2.5 grams)
- 2 tablespoons olive oil (30 ml)
- 1 tablespoon chopped fresh cilantro (4 grams)
- 1 tablespoon chopped fresh mint (4 grams)
- 1 lemon, juiced (about 50 ml)

Directions:

1. In a large bowl, mix together the garlic, cumin, paprika, turmeric, coriander, cinnamon, chili powder, salt, pepper, olive oil, cilantro, mint, and lemon juice. Add the cubed lamb and toss until well coated. Cover the bowl with plastic wrap and marinate in the refrigerator for at least 2 hours or overnight for best results.
2. Preheat the grill to medium-high heat. Remove the lamb from the refrigerator and thread the cubes onto skewers, leaving a small space between each piece of meat.
3. Place the skewers on the preheated grill and cook for about 4-5 minutes on each side, turning once, until the lamb is cooked to your desired level of doneness.
4. Remove the kebabs from the grill and let them rest for a few minutes before serving.

Nutritional Information: Estimated per serving: 400 calories, 28 grams protein, 3 grams carbohydrates, 30 grams fat, 1 gram fiber, 95 milligrams cholesterol, 650 milligrams sodium, 300 milligrams potassium.

Garlic Parmesan Crusted Pork Tenderloin

Yield: 4 servings | Prep time: 15 minutes | Cook time: 30 minutes

Ingredients:

- 600 grams pork tenderloin
- 2 tablespoons olive oil (30 ml)
- 1 teaspoon salt (5 grams)
- 1/2 teaspoon black pepper (2.5 grams)
- 4 garlic cloves, minced (about 12 grams)
- 1 teaspoon dried rosemary (1 gram)
- 1 teaspoon dried thyme (1 gram)
- 1/2 cup grated Parmesan cheese (45 grams)
- 1/4 cup almond flour (28 grams)
- 2 tablespoons chopped fresh parsley (8 grams)

Directions:

1. Preheat your oven to 180°C (350°F). In a small bowl, mix together the olive oil, salt, pepper, minced garlic, rosemary, and thyme.
2. Pat the pork tenderloin dry with paper towels and rub the spice mixture all over the meat. Place the tenderloin on a baking sheet lined with parchment paper or aluminum foil.
3. In another small bowl, combine the grated Parmesan cheese and almond flour. Press this mixture onto the top and sides of the pork tenderloin, covering it evenly.
4. Roast the pork in the preheated oven for about 25-30 minutes, or until it reaches an internal temperature of 63°C (145°F). Let it rest for 5 minutes before slicing.
5. Sprinkle the sliced pork with fresh parsley and serve.

Nutritional Information: Estimated per serving: 340 calories, 38 grams protein, 3 grams carbohydrates, 19 grams fat, 1 gram fiber, 110 milligrams cholesterol, 720 milligrams sodium, 500 milligrams potassium.

Bacon-Wrapped Stuffed Chicken

Yield: 4 servings | Prep time: 15 minutes | Cook time: 35 minutes

Ingredients:

- 4 boneless, skinless chicken breasts (about 600 grams)
- 8 rashers of bacon (about 240 grams)
- 100 grams cream cheese, softened
- 50 grams grated cheddar cheese
- 1/4 cup chopped fresh spinach (about 30 grams)
- 1/4 cup chopped sun-dried tomatoes (about 30 grams)
- 2 cloves garlic, minced (about 6 grams)
- 1/2 teaspoon salt (2.5 grams)
- 1/4 teaspoon black pepper (1.25 grams)
- 1 tablespoon olive oil (15 ml)

Directions:

1. Preheat your oven to 200°C (400°F). In a medium bowl, mix together the cream cheese, cheddar cheese, spinach, sun-dried tomatoes, garlic, salt, and pepper. Set aside.
2. Place each chicken breast between two pieces of plastic wrap and use a meat mallet or rolling pin to flatten them to an even thickness of about 1.5 cm.
3. Spread the cream cheese mixture evenly over each chicken breast, leaving a small border around the edges. Roll up each chicken breast tightly and wrap with two rashers of bacon, securing with toothpicks if needed.
4. Heat the olive oil in a large, ovenproof skillet over medium-high heat. Add the bacon-wrapped chicken breasts and sear until the bacon is browned on all sides, about 2-3 minutes per side.
5. Transfer the skillet to the preheated oven and bake for 20-25 minutes, or until the chicken is cooked through and no longer pink in the center.
6. Remove from the oven and let the chicken rest for a few minutes before slicing and serving.

Nutritional Information: Estimated per serving: 470 calories, 40 grams protein, 4 grams carbohydrates, 32 grams fat, 0.5 grams fiber, 120 milligrams cholesterol, 850 milligrams sodium, 500 milligrams potassium.

Slow Cooker Keto Pulled Pork

Yield: 6 servings | Prep time: 15 minutes | Cook time: 480 minutes

Ingredients:

- 1.5 kg pork shoulder (boneless)
- 1 tablespoon smoked paprika (15 grams)
- 2 teaspoons garlic powder (10 grams)
- 2 teaspoons onion powder (10 grams)
- 1 teaspoon cayenne pepper (5 grams)
- 1 teaspoon ground cumin (5 grams)
- 1 teaspoon salt (5 grams)
- 1/2 teaspoon black pepper (2.5 grams)
- 1/4 cup chicken broth (60 ml)
- 2 tablespoons apple cider vinegar (30 ml)
- 2 tablespoons Worcestershire sauce (30 ml)

Directions:

1. In a small bowl, mix together the smoked paprika, garlic powder, onion powder, cayenne pepper, cumin, salt, and black pepper. Rub the spice mixture all over the pork shoulder, making sure to coat it evenly.
2. In a slow cooker, combine the chicken broth, apple cider vinegar, and Worcestershire sauce. Place the seasoned pork shoulder in the slow cooker, making sure it's submerged in the liquid.
3. Cover and cook on low for 8 hours, or until the pork is tender and easily shreds with a fork.
4. Once the pork is cooked, remove it from the slow cooker and shred it using two forks. Return the shredded pork to the slow cooker and mix it with the remaining liquid to keep it moist and flavorful.
5. Serve the pulled pork on its own, or use it as a filling for lettuce wraps, keto-friendly tacos, or salads.

Nutritional Information: Estimated per serving: 380 calories, 50 grams protein, 2 grams carbohydrates, 17 grams fat, 0.5 grams fiber, 145 milligrams cholesterol, 550 milligrams sodium, 700 milligrams potassium.

Cajun Chicken Alfredo

Yield: 4 servings | Prep time: 15 minutes | Cook time: 20 minutes

Ingredients:

- 4 boneless, skinless chicken breasts (about 600 grams)
- 2 tablespoons Cajun seasoning (30 grams)
- 2 tablespoons olive oil (30 ml)
- 4 cloves garlic, minced (12 grams)
- 1 cup heavy cream (240 ml)
- 1 cup grated Parmesan cheese (100 grams)
- 1/4 teaspoon salt (1.25 grams)
- 1/4 teaspoon black pepper (1.25 grams)
- 2 tablespoons chopped fresh parsley (30 grams)
- 1 tablespoon lemon juice (15 ml)

Directions:

1. Season the chicken breasts on both sides with the Cajun seasoning. In a large skillet, heat the olive oil over medium-high heat. Add the chicken breasts and cook for about 5-6 minutes on each side, or until fully cooked and golden brown. Remove the chicken from the skillet and set it aside.
2. In the same skillet, add the minced garlic and sauté for 1 minute, or until fragrant. Add the heavy cream, Parmesan cheese, salt, and pepper. Cook, stirring continuously, until the cheese has melted and the sauce has thickened.
3. Slice the cooked chicken breasts and add them back to the skillet. Stir in the parsley and lemon juice, and cook for an additional 2-3 minutes, or until heated through.
4. Serve the Cajun chicken Alfredo hot, garnished with additional parsley and Parmesan cheese, if desired.

Nutritional Information: Estimated per serving: 420 calories, 35 grams protein, 5 grams carbohydrates, 28 grams fat, 0.5 grams fiber, 150 milligrams cholesterol, 630 milligrams sodium, 450 milligrams potassium.

Baked Lemon Herb Chicken Thighs

Yield: 4 servings | Prep time: 10 minutes | Cook time: 40 minutes

Ingredients:

- 4 bone-in, skin-on chicken thighs (about 800 grams)
- 2 tablespoons olive oil (30 ml)
- 4 cloves garlic, minced (12 grams)
- 1 teaspoon dried thyme (2 grams)
- 1 teaspoon dried oregano (2 grams)
- 1 teaspoon dried basil (2 grams)
- 1/2 teaspoon salt (2.5 grams)
- 1/4 teaspoon black pepper (1.25 grams)
- Zest and juice of 1 lemon
- 1/2 cup chicken broth (120 ml)

Directions:

1. Preheat your oven to 190°C (375°F). In a small bowl, mix together the olive oil, garlic, thyme, oregano, basil, salt, pepper, lemon zest, and lemon juice. Set aside.
2. In a large oven-safe skillet, heat a small amount of oil over medium heat. Add the chicken thighs, skin-side down, and sear for about 3-4 minutes or until the skin is golden brown. Flip the thighs over and sear for an additional 3-4 minutes.
3. Remove the skillet from heat, and pour the lemon herb mixture over the chicken thighs. Pour the chicken broth into the skillet, avoiding the tops of the chicken thighs.
4. Place the skillet in the oven and bake for 30-35 minutes or until the chicken is cooked through and the internal temperature reaches 75°C (165°F).
5. Serve the chicken thighs hot with the pan juices spooned over the top.

Nutritional Information: Estimated per serving: 330 calories, 28 grams protein, 3 grams carbohydrates, 22 grams fat, 1 gram fiber, 120 milligrams cholesterol, 410 milligrams sodium, 320 milligrams potassium.

Herb-Crusted Rack of Lamb

Yield: 4 servings | Prep time: 10 minutes | Cook time: 25 minutes

Ingredients:

- 1 rack of lamb (about 800 grams)
- 3 tablespoons olive oil (45 ml)
- 4 cloves garlic, minced (12 grams)
- 2 tablespoons fresh rosemary, chopped (6 grams)
- 2 tablespoons fresh thyme, chopped (6 grams)
- 1 tablespoon fresh parsley, chopped (3 grams)
- 1 teaspoon salt (5 grams)
- 1/2 teaspoon black pepper (2.5 grams)
- 1/4 cup almond flour (30 grams)

Directions:

1. Preheat your oven to 220°C (425°F). In a small bowl, mix together the olive oil, garlic, rosemary, thyme, parsley, salt, and pepper. Set aside.
2. In a large oven-safe skillet, heat a small amount of oil over medium-high heat. Add the rack of lamb, fat-side down, and sear for about 3-4 minutes or until the fat is golden brown. Flip the rack over and sear for an additional 1-2 minutes.
3. Remove the skillet from heat, and spread the herb mixture over the fat side of the rack of lamb. Sprinkle the almond flour over the top, pressing it into the herb mixture to create a crust.
4. Place the skillet in the oven and roast for 15-20 minutes or until the internal temperature of the lamb reaches 57°C (135°F) for medium-rare. Remove the skillet from the oven and let the lamb rest for 5 minutes.
5. Slice the rack of lamb into individual chops and serve.

Nutritional Information: Estimated per serving: 425 calories, 33 grams protein, 2 grams carbohydrates, 32 grams fat, 1 gram fiber, 105 milligrams cholesterol, 620 milligrams sodium, 360 milligrams potassium.

Vegetarian and Vegan Options on Keto

Spinach and Feta Stuffed Portobello Mushrooms

Yield: 4 servings | Prep time: 10 minutes | Cook time: 25 minutes

Ingredients:

- 4 large portobello mushrooms (about 400 grams)
- 2 tablespoons olive oil (30 ml)
- 1 small onion, chopped (about 70 grams)
- 2 cloves garlic, minced (6 grams)
- 200 grams fresh spinach
- 100 grams feta cheese, crumbled
- 1/4 teaspoon salt (1.25 grams)
- 1/4 teaspoon black pepper (1.25 grams)
- 1/4 teaspoon red pepper flakes (optional) (0.5 grams)

Directions:

1. Preheat your oven to 190°C (375°F). Remove the stems from the portobello mushrooms and scrape out the gills with a spoon. Brush the mushrooms with 1 tablespoon of olive oil and place them on a baking sheet, stem-side up.
2. In a large skillet, heat the remaining tablespoon of olive oil over medium heat. Add the onion and garlic and sauté for 2-3 minutes until the onion is soft. Add the spinach and cook until it wilts, about 2-3 minutes. Remove the skillet from heat and stir in the feta cheese, salt, pepper, and red pepper flakes.
3. Divide the spinach and feta mixture among the four mushrooms, pressing it into the caps. Bake for 20-25 minutes or until the mushrooms are tender and the cheese is golden brown.
4. Serve the stuffed mushrooms hot.

Nutritional Information: Estimated per serving: 160 calories, 6 grams protein, 9 grams carbohydrates, 12 grams fat, 3 grams fiber, 25 milligrams cholesterol, 490 milligrams sodium, 610 milligrams potassium.

Cheesy Cauliflower Bake

Yield: 4 servings | Prep time: 10 minutes | Cook time: 35 minutes

Ingredients:

- 1 large head of cauliflower (800 grams), cut into florets
- 2 tablespoons olive oil (30 ml)
- Salt and pepper, to taste
- 3/4 cup heavy cream (180 ml)
- 2 cups shredded cheddar cheese (200 grams)
- 1/4 cup grated Parmesan cheese (30 grams)
- 1/4 teaspoon garlic powder (0.6 grams)
- 1/4 teaspoon dried oregano (0.25 grams)
- 2 tablespoons chopped fresh parsley (8 grams)

Directions:

1. Preheat your oven to 200°C (390°F). Place the cauliflower florets in a baking dish, drizzle with olive oil, and season with salt and pepper. Toss to coat the cauliflower evenly, then spread them out in a single layer.
2. Bake the cauliflower for 15 minutes, until it starts to soften and turn slightly golden.
3. In a medium saucepan, heat the heavy cream over medium heat until it begins to simmer. Reduce the heat to low and add 1 1/2 cups of cheddar cheese, the Parmesan cheese, garlic powder, and oregano. Stir until the cheese is melted and the sauce is smooth.
4. Pour the cheese sauce over the cauliflower, then sprinkle the remaining 1/2 cup of cheddar cheese on top.
5. Bake for an additional 20 minutes, until the cheese is melted and bubbly, and the cauliflower is tender.
6. Sprinkle with chopped parsley before serving.

Nutritional Information: Estimated per serving: 450 calories, 18 grams protein, 10 grams carbohydrates, 39 grams fat, 3 grams fiber, 110 milligrams cholesterol, 520 milligrams sodium, 670 milligrams potassium.

Keto Eggplant Parmesan
Yield: 4 servings | Prep time: 15 minutes | Cook time: 45 minutes

Ingredients:

- 2 medium eggplants (about 600 grams)
- 1 teaspoon salt (5 grams)
- 3 tablespoons olive oil (45 ml)
- 1/2 cup almond flour (60 grams)
- 1/4 cup grated Parmesan cheese (30 grams)
- 1/4 teaspoon black pepper (1.25 grams)
- 1/2 teaspoon garlic powder (1.5 grams)
- 1/2 teaspoon dried oregano (1 gram)

- 1 large egg (50 grams)
- 1 tablespoon water (15 ml)
- 1 cup marinara sauce, no sugar added (240 ml)
- 1 1/2 cups shredded mozzarella cheese (170 grams)
- 2 tablespoons chopped fresh basil (8 grams)

Directions:

1. Preheat your oven to 220°C (425°F). Cut the eggplants into 1/2-inch (1.3 cm) slices and sprinkle both sides with salt. Place them in a colander for 10 minutes to remove excess moisture.
2. In a shallow dish, mix almond flour, Parmesan cheese, black pepper, garlic powder, and oregano. In another shallow dish, whisk together the egg and water.
3. Dip each eggplant slice in the egg mixture, letting excess drip off, then coat with the almond flour mixture, pressing it onto the eggplant. Place the slices in a single layer on a baking sheet lined with parchment paper.
4. Drizzle the eggplant slices with olive oil and bake for 20 minutes, flipping halfway through, until golden brown.
5. Spread 1/2 cup of marinara sauce in the bottom of a baking dish. Layer half of the eggplant slices on top, then spread another 1/2 cup of sauce over them. Sprinkle 1 cup of mozzarella cheese over the sauce.
6. Repeat with the remaining eggplant, sauce, and cheese. Bake for 25 minutes until the cheese is melted and bubbly. Garnish with chopped basil before serving.

Nutritional Information: Estimated per serving: 320 calories, 13 grams protein, 14 grams carbohydrates, 25 grams fat, 6 grams fiber, 55 milligrams cholesterol, 890 milligrams sodium, 670 milligrams potassium.

Zucchini Noodles with Pesto and Sun-dried Tomatoes
Yield: 4 servings | Prep time: 15 minutes | Cook time: 5 minutes

Ingredients:

- 4 medium zucchini (800 grams), spiralized into noodles
- 2 tablespoons olive oil (30 ml)
- 1/2 cup pesto sauce (125 ml)
- 1/2 cup sun-dried tomatoes, chopped (65 grams)

- 1/2 cup cherry tomatoes, halved (75 grams)
- 1/4 cup pine nuts, toasted (30 grams)
- 2 tablespoons nutritional yeast (15 grams)
- 1 clove garlic, minced (3 grams)
- Salt and pepper, to taste
- Fresh basil, for garnish

Directions:

1. Heat the olive oil in a large skillet over medium heat. Add the minced garlic and sauté for 1 minute, until fragrant.
2. Add the spiralized zucchini noodles to the skillet and sauté for 3-4 minutes, until slightly softened.
3. Stir in the pesto sauce, sun-dried tomatoes, cherry tomatoes, pine nuts, and nutritional yeast. Season with salt and pepper to taste.
4. Toss the ingredients until well combined and heated through, about 1-2 minutes.
5. Serve the zucchini noodles hot, garnished with fresh basil.

Nutritional Information: Estimated per serving: 260 calories, 7 grams protein, 13 grams carbohydrates, 21 grams fat, 5 grams fiber, 0 milligrams cholesterol, 220 milligrams sodium, 420 milligrams potassium.

Creamy Avocado Spinach Spaghetti Squash

Yield: 4 servings | Prep time: 15 minutes | Cook time: 40 minutes

Ingredients:

- 1 medium spaghetti squash (about 1.5 kg)
- 2 tablespoons olive oil (30 ml)
- Salt and pepper, to taste
- 2 ripe avocados (400 grams)
- 2 cups baby spinach (60 grams)
- 2 cloves garlic (6 grams)
- 1/4 cup fresh basil leaves (10 grams)
- 2 tablespoons lemon juice (30 ml)
- 1/4 cup grated Parmesan cheese (30 grams)
- 1/4 teaspoon crushed red pepper flakes (0.5 grams)

Directions:

1. Preheat your oven to 200°C (390°F). Cut the spaghetti squash in half lengthwise and remove the seeds. Drizzle the inside with olive oil and season with salt and pepper. Place the squash cut side down on a baking sheet and bake for 35-40 minutes until tender.
2. While the squash is baking, prepare the sauce. In a food processor, combine avocados, spinach, garlic, basil, lemon juice, and half of the Parmesan cheese. Process until smooth and creamy. Season with salt and pepper to taste.
3. Once the squash is cooked, let it cool for a few minutes. Then, use a fork to scrape the flesh into spaghetti-like strands.
4. In a large mixing bowl, combine the spaghetti squash and the avocado-spinach sauce. Toss until the squash is well coated.
5. Divide the squash among serving plates and sprinkle with the remaining Parmesan cheese and red pepper flakes.

Nutritional Information: Estimated per serving: 280 calories, 7 grams protein, 18 grams carbohydrates, 22 grams fat, 9 grams fiber, 5 milligrams cholesterol, 220 milligrams sodium, 830 milligrams potassium.

Roasted Red Pepper and Tomato Soup

Yield: 4 servings | Prep time: 10 minutes | Cook time: 35 minutes

Ingredients:

- 4 large red bell peppers (600 grams)
- 6 medium tomatoes (600 grams)
- 2 tablespoons olive oil (30 ml)
- 1 medium onion, diced (150 grams)
- 3 cloves garlic, minced (9 grams)
- 1/4 teaspoon smoked paprika (0.5 grams)
- 1/4 teaspoon ground cumin (0.5 grams)
- 1/4 teaspoon chili flakes (0.5 grams)
- Salt and pepper, to taste
- 3 cups chicken or vegetable broth (720 ml)
- 1/2 cup heavy cream (120 ml)
- Fresh basil leaves, for garnish

Directions:

1. Preheat your oven to 220°C (425°F). Line a baking tray with parchment paper. Place the red peppers and tomatoes on the tray and drizzle with 1 tablespoon of olive oil. Roast for 25 minutes or until the skins are slightly charred and the vegetables are tender.
2. While the vegetables are roasting, heat the remaining olive oil in a large pot over medium heat. Add the onions and garlic, and sauté until soft and translucent, about 5 minutes.
3. Once the vegetables are roasted, remove the skins and seeds from the peppers and the skins from the tomatoes. Chop the vegetables into smaller pieces and add them to the pot with the onions and garlic.
4. Add the smoked paprika, cumin, chili flakes, salt, and pepper to the pot. Pour in the broth and bring to a simmer. Cook for 10 minutes to allow the flavors to meld.
5. Use an immersion blender to purée the soup until smooth. Stir in the heavy cream and heat through. Taste and adjust the seasoning as needed.
6. Serve the soup hot, garnished with fresh basil leaves.

Nutritional Information: Estimated per serving: 240 calories, 4 grams protein, 18 grams carbohydrates, 18 grams fat, 5 grams fiber, 40 milligrams cholesterol, 600 milligrams sodium, 700 milligrams potassium.

Vegan Keto Thai Curry

Yield: 4 servings | Prep time: 15 minutes | Cook time: 20 minutes

Ingredients:

- 1 tablespoon coconut oil (15 ml)
- 1 medium onion, diced (150 grams)
- 3 cloves garlic, minced (9 grams)
- 1 tablespoon ginger, minced (15 grams)
- 1 tablespoon Thai red curry paste (15 grams)
- 1 can full-fat coconut milk (400 ml)
- 200 grams tofu, cubed
- 200 grams broccoli florets
- 150 grams red bell pepper, sliced
- 150 grams green bell pepper, sliced
- 2 tablespoons tamari or soy sauce (30 ml)
- 2 tablespoons lime juice (30 ml)
- 1 tablespoon erythritol or another keto-friendly sweetener (15 grams)
- Fresh coriander, chopped, for garnish
- Red chili flakes, optional, for garnish

Directions:

1. Heat the coconut oil in a large pan over medium heat. Add the onion, garlic, and ginger, and sauté until soft and translucent, about 5 minutes.
2. Stir in the red curry paste and cook for an additional minute, until fragrant.
3. Pour in the coconut milk, tamari, lime juice, and erythritol. Bring to a simmer, stirring occasionally to dissolve the erythritol.
4. Add the tofu, broccoli, and bell peppers to the pan. Simmer for 10 minutes or until the vegetables are tender.
5. Taste the curry and adjust the seasoning as needed. Remove from heat.
6. Serve the curry hot, garnished with fresh coriander and chili flakes.

Nutritional Information: Estimated per serving: 290 calories, 8 grams protein, 10 grams carbohydrates, 25 grams fat, 3 grams fiber, 0 milligrams cholesterol, 420 milligrams sodium, 400 milligrams potassium.

Cauliflower Tabbouleh Salad

Yield: 4 servings | Prep time: 20 minutes | Cook time: 0 minutes

Ingredients:

- 1 small cauliflower head, riced (about 500 grams)
- 1 large cucumber, diced (about 150 grams)
- 4 ripe tomatoes, diced (about 400 grams)
- 1 small red onion, finely chopped (about 70 grams)
- 1 cup fresh parsley, chopped (about 30 grams)
- 1/2 cup fresh mint, chopped (about 20 grams)
- 3 tablespoons extra virgin olive oil (45 ml)
- 2 tablespoons lemon juice (30 ml)
- Salt and pepper, to taste

Directions:

1. In a large mixing bowl, combine the riced cauliflower, diced cucumber, diced tomatoes, chopped red onion, chopped parsley, and chopped mint.
2. In a small bowl, whisk together the olive oil, lemon juice, salt, and pepper.
3. Pour the dressing over the cauliflower mixture and toss well to combine.
4. Refrigerate the tabbouleh for at least 1 hour before serving to allow the flavors to meld.
5. Serve the cauliflower tabbouleh as a side dish or a light, refreshing salad.

Nutritional Information: Estimated per serving: 150 calories, 4 grams protein, 15 grams carbohydrates, 10 grams fat, 4 grams fiber, 0 milligrams cholesterol, 60 milligrams sodium, 600 milligrams potassium.

Vegan Keto Pad Thai

Yield: 4 servings | Prep time: 15 minutes | Cook time: 20 minutes

Ingredients:

- 400 grams shirataki noodles (keto-friendly, low-carb noodles)
- 1 tablespoon coconut oil (15 ml)
- 1 medium red bell pepper, thinly sliced (about 150 grams)
- 1 medium zucchini, julienned (about 200 grams)
- 3 spring onions, thinly sliced (about 30 grams)
- 200 grams firm tofu, cubed
- 2 tablespoons almond butter (30 ml)
- 2 tablespoons tamari sauce (30 ml)
- 2 tablespoons lime juice (30 ml)
- 1 tablespoon Sriracha sauce (15 ml)
- 2 cloves garlic, minced
- 1 teaspoon ginger, minced
- 2 tablespoons fresh coriander, chopped (about 10 grams)
- 2 tablespoons crushed peanuts (about 30 grams)
- 1 lime, cut into wedges

Directions:

1. Rinse the shirataki noodles in cold water and drain well. Set aside.
2. In a large frying pan or wok, heat the coconut oil over medium heat. Add the tofu cubes and cook until golden brown, about 8 minutes. Remove from the pan and set aside.
3. In the same pan, add the red bell pepper, zucchini, and spring onions. Cook for about 5 minutes until the vegetables are tender.
4. In a small bowl, mix the almond butter, tamari sauce, lime juice, Sriracha sauce, garlic, and ginger until smooth.
5. Add the sauce to the pan along with the shirataki noodles and tofu. Toss everything to combine and cook for another 5 minutes until heated through.
6. Serve the Vegan Keto Pad Thai garnished with fresh coriander, crushed peanuts, and lime wedges.

Nutritional Information: Estimated per serving: 210 calories, 10 grams protein, 8 grams carbohydrates, 16 grams fat, 3 grams fiber, 0 milligrams cholesterol, 680 milligrams sodium, 400 milligrams potassium.

Avocado and Walnut Salad

Yield: 4 servings | Prep time: 10 minutes | Cook time: 0 minutes

Ingredients:

- 2 large avocados, diced (about 300 grams)
- 100 grams walnuts, roughly chopped
- 100 grams feta cheese, crumbled
- 50 grams rocket (arugula) leaves
- 1 small red onion, thinly sliced (about 50 grams)
- 2 tablespoons olive oil (30 ml)
- 1 tablespoon balsamic vinegar (15 ml)
- 1/2 teaspoon salt (2 grams)
- 1/4 teaspoon black pepper (1 gram)
- 1/2 teaspoon Dijon mustard (2 grams)

Directions:

1. In a large salad bowl, combine the rocket leaves, avocado, walnuts, feta cheese, and red onion.
2. In a small bowl, whisk together the olive oil, balsamic vinegar, salt, black pepper, and Dijon mustard until well combined.
3. Drizzle the dressing over the salad and toss gently to combine.
4. Serve the salad immediately as a light meal or as a side dish.

Nutritional Information: Estimated per serving: 330 calories, 9 grams protein, 11 grams carbohydrates, 30 grams fat, 7 grams fiber, 25 milligrams cholesterol, 540 milligrams sodium, 590 milligrams potassium.

Spinach and Artichoke Dip

Yield: 6 servings | Prep time: 10 minutes | Cook time: 25 minutes

Ingredients:

- 200 grams fresh spinach, chopped
- 1 can (400 grams) artichoke hearts, drained and chopped
- 200 grams cream cheese, softened
- 100 grams mayonnaise
- 100 grams sour cream
- 100 grams grated Parmesan cheese
- 100 grams grated mozzarella cheese
- 3 cloves garlic, minced
- 1 teaspoon salt (5 grams)
- 1/2 teaspoon black pepper (2 grams)
- 1/4 teaspoon crushed red pepper flakes (1 gram)
- 1 tablespoon olive oil for greasing (15 ml)

Directions:

1. Preheat the oven to 180°C (350°F). Grease a baking dish with olive oil.
2. In a large mixing bowl, combine the cream cheese, mayonnaise, sour cream, half of the Parmesan cheese, half of the mozzarella cheese, garlic, salt, black pepper, and red pepper flakes. Mix well until smooth.
3. Fold in the chopped spinach and artichoke hearts until they are evenly distributed throughout the mixture.
4. Transfer the mixture to the prepared baking dish and spread it out evenly.
5. Sprinkle the remaining Parmesan and mozzarella cheeses on top of the mixture.
6. Bake in the preheated oven for 25 minutes, or until the dip is hot and bubbly and the cheese on top has melted and turned golden brown.
7. Serve the Spinach and Artichoke Dip hot with keto-friendly crackers or vegetables for dipping.

Nutritional Information: Estimated per serving: 380 calories, 10 grams protein, 8 grams carbohydrates, 35 grams fat, 3 grams fiber, 80 milligrams cholesterol, 700 milligrams sodium, 350 milligrams potassium.

Vegan Keto Coconut Curry

Yield: 4 servings | Prep time: 15 minutes | Cook time: 25 minutes

Ingredients:

- 400 grams canned coconut milk (full fat)
- 300 grams cauliflower florets
- 200 grams broccoli florets
- 200 grams mushrooms, sliced
- 150 grams spinach leaves
- 1 red bell pepper, sliced (about 150 grams)
- 1 medium onion, chopped (about 150 grams)
- 3 cloves garlic, minced (about 9 grams)
- 1 tablespoon curry powder (8 grams)
- 1 teaspoon ground turmeric (3 grams)
- 1 teaspoon ground cumin (2 grams)
- 1 teaspoon chili powder (2 grams)
- 1 teaspoon salt (5 grams)
- 2 tablespoons olive oil (30 ml)
- Fresh coriander leaves, for garnish

Directions:

1. In a large skillet or wok, heat the olive oil over medium heat. Add the onion and garlic, and sauté until softened and translucent, about 3-5 minutes.
2. Stir in the curry powder, turmeric, cumin, chili powder, and salt. Cook for 1-2 minutes, until the spices are fragrant.
3. Add the coconut milk to the skillet and bring to a gentle simmer. Add the cauliflower, broccoli, mushrooms, and red bell pepper. Cook, stirring occasionally, for about 15 minutes, or until the vegetables are tender.
4. Stir in the spinach and cook for another 2 minutes, until wilted.
5. Serve the curry over cauliflower rice or on its own, garnished with fresh coriander leaves.

Nutritional Information: Estimated per serving: 280 calories, 6 grams protein, 16 grams carbohydrates, 23 grams fat, 6 grams fiber, 0 milligrams cholesterol, 650 milligrams sodium, 850 milligrams potassium.

Creamy Vegan Broccoli Soup

Yield: 4 servings | Prep time: 10 minutes | Cook time: 25 minutes

Ingredients:

- 400 grams broccoli florets
- 400 ml canned coconut milk (full fat)
- 1 medium onion, chopped (about 150 grams)
- 3 cloves garlic, minced (about 9 grams)
- 750 ml vegetable broth
- 2 tablespoons olive oil (30 ml)
- 1 teaspoon salt (5 grams)
- 1/2 teaspoon black pepper (1 gram)
- 1 teaspoon dried thyme (1 gram)
- 1/4 teaspoon red pepper flakes (optional) (0.5 grams)
- Fresh parsley, for garnish

Directions:

1. In a large pot, heat the olive oil over medium heat. Add the onion and garlic, and sauté until softened and translucent, about 3-5 minutes.
2. Add the broccoli florets, vegetable broth, salt, black pepper, thyme, and red pepper flakes (if using). Bring to a boil, then reduce the heat to low, cover, and simmer for about 15 minutes, or until the broccoli is tender.
3. Remove the pot from the heat and use an immersion blender to puree the soup until smooth. Alternatively, transfer the soup to a blender and blend in batches, then return to the pot.
4. Stir in the coconut milk and return to the heat. Simmer for an additional 5 minutes, or until heated through.
5. Serve the soup hot, garnished with fresh parsley.

Nutritional Information: Estimated per serving: 280 calories, 4 grams protein, 16 grams carbohydrates, 23 grams fat, 5 grams fiber, 0 milligrams cholesterol, 950 milligrams sodium, 550 milligrams potassium.

Vegan Stuffed Bell Peppers

Yield: 4 servings | Prep time: 15 minutes | Cook time: 45 minutes

Ingredients:

- 4 large bell peppers (any color), tops removed and seeds discarded (about 600 grams)
- 200 grams cauliflower rice (raw)
- 150 grams mushrooms, chopped
- 100 grams spinach, chopped
- 1 medium onion, chopped (about 150 grams)
- 3 cloves garlic, minced (about 9 grams)
- 400 ml canned diced tomatoes
- 2 tablespoons olive oil (30 ml)
- 1 teaspoon smoked paprika (2 grams)
- 1 teaspoon ground cumin (2 grams)
- 1/2 teaspoon ground black pepper (1 gram)
- 1/2 teaspoon salt (2.5 grams)
- Fresh parsley, for garnish

Directions:

1. Preheat your oven to 200°C (390°F). Grease a baking dish and set aside.
2. In a large skillet, heat the olive oil over medium heat. Add the onions and garlic, and sauté until softened and translucent, about 3-5 minutes.
3. Add the mushrooms, spinach, smoked paprika, ground cumin, salt, and pepper to the skillet. Sauté until the mushrooms are cooked and the spinach is wilted, about 5 minutes.
4. Stir in the cauliflower rice and canned diced tomatoes. Cook for an additional 5 minutes, allowing the flavors to meld together.
5. Spoon the mixture into the hollowed-out bell peppers, pressing down gently to compact the filling. Place the stuffed peppers in the prepared baking dish.
6. Cover the baking dish with foil and bake in the preheated oven for 30 minutes, or until the peppers are tender.
7. Remove from the oven and let cool for a few minutes. Garnish with fresh parsley before serving.

Nutritional Information: Estimated per serving: 160 calories, 4 grams protein, 20 grams carbohydrates, 8 grams fat, 6 grams fiber, 0 milligrams cholesterol, 450 milligrams sodium, 650 milligrams potassium.

Marinated Grilled Eggplant

Yield: 4 servings | Prep time: 15 minutes | Cook time: 10 minutes

Ingredients:

- 2 large eggplants (about 500 grams), sliced into 1 cm thick rounds
- 60 ml extra virgin olive oil
- 2 tablespoons balsamic vinegar (30 ml)
- 3 cloves garlic, minced (about 9 grams)
- 1 teaspoon dried oregano (1 gram)
- 1 teaspoon dried basil (1 gram)
- 1/2 teaspoon salt (2.5 grams)
- 1/4 teaspoon ground black pepper (0.5 grams)
- Fresh parsley or basil leaves, for garnish

Directions:

1. In a medium bowl, whisk together the olive oil, balsamic vinegar, garlic, oregano, basil, salt, and black pepper.
2. Place the eggplant slices in a large dish or zip-top bag. Pour the marinade over the eggplant slices, ensuring each slice is coated. Allow the eggplant to marinate for at least 30 minutes, turning occasionally to redistribute the marinade.
3. Preheat your grill or grill pan to medium-high heat. Remove the eggplant slices from the marinade and grill for about 3-5 minutes per side, until the eggplant is tender and has grill marks.
4. Remove the eggplant slices from the grill and arrange them on a serving platter. Garnish with fresh parsley or basil leaves before serving.

Nutritional Information: Estimated per serving: 190 calories, 2 grams protein, 12 grams carbohydrates, 15 grams fat, 5 grams fiber, 0 milligrams cholesterol, 300 milligrams sodium, 400 milligrams potassium.

Soups, Salads, and Sides: Perfect Keto Companions

Creamy Cauliflower Soup

Yield: 4 servings | Prep time: 10 minutes | Cook time: 25 minutes

Ingredients:

- 1 medium cauliflower (about 500 grams), cut into florets
- 2 tablespoons olive oil (30 ml)
- 1 small onion, diced (about 70 grams)
- 3 cloves garlic, minced (about 9 grams)
- 500 ml vegetable broth
- 200 ml coconut cream
- 1/2 teaspoon salt (2.5 grams)
- 1/4 teaspoon black pepper (0.5 grams)
- 1/2 teaspoon dried thyme (0.5 grams)
- Fresh chives, for garnish

Directions:

1. In a large pot, heat the olive oil over medium heat. Add the diced onion and sauté until translucent, about 5 minutes. Add the minced garlic and sauté for another 2 minutes.
2. Add the cauliflower florets to the pot, along with the vegetable broth, salt, pepper, and thyme. Bring the mixture to a boil, then reduce the heat to low and simmer for about 15 minutes, or until the cauliflower is tender.
3. Use an immersion blender to puree the soup until smooth, or transfer the soup to a blender and blend in batches until smooth.
4. Return the soup to the pot and stir in the coconut cream. Heat the soup over low heat until warmed through.
5. Serve the soup in bowls, garnished with fresh chives.

Nutritional Information: Estimated per serving: 260 calories, 4 grams protein, 11 grams carbohydrates, 23 grams fat, 3 grams fiber, 0 milligrams cholesterol, 500 milligrams sodium, 400 milligrams potassium.

Spinach, Bacon, and Egg Salad

Yield: 4 servings | Prep time: 10 minutes | Cook time: 10 minutes

Ingredients:

- 200 grams fresh spinach
- 4 large eggs
- 200 grams bacon
- 1 small red onion, thinly sliced (about 70 grams)
- 100 grams cherry tomatoes, halved
- 2 tablespoons extra-virgin olive oil (30 ml)
- 1 tablespoon white wine vinegar (15 ml)
- 1/2 teaspoon Dijon mustard (2.5 grams)
- 1/4 teaspoon salt (1.25 grams)
- 1/4 teaspoon black pepper (0.5 grams)

Directions:

1. Place the eggs in a saucepan and cover with water. Bring to a boil over high heat. Once boiling, reduce heat to low and simmer for 9 minutes. Remove from heat and transfer eggs to a bowl of ice water to cool. Once cooled, peel and halve the eggs.
2. In a large skillet, cook the bacon over medium heat until crispy, about 8-10 minutes. Remove from the skillet and drain on paper towels. Once cooled, chop into bite-sized pieces.
3. In a large bowl, combine the spinach, sliced onion, and halved tomatoes. Add the halved eggs and chopped bacon.
4. In a small bowl, whisk together the olive oil, vinegar, mustard, salt, and pepper. Drizzle the dressing over the salad and toss to coat.
5. Serve the salad in individual bowls.

Nutritional Information: Estimated per serving: 295 calories, 12 grams protein, 4 grams carbohydrates, 25 grams fat, 2 grams fiber, 205 milligrams cholesterol, 590 milligrams sodium, 370 milligrams potassium.

Parmesan Roasted Brussels Sprouts

Yield: 4 servings | Prep time: 10 minutes | Cook time: 25 minutes

Ingredients:

- 500 grams Brussels sprouts, trimmed and halved
- 3 tablespoons olive oil (45 ml)
- 1/2 teaspoon salt (2.5 grams)
- 1/4 teaspoon black pepper (0.5 grams)
- 60 grams grated Parmesan cheese
- 2 cloves garlic, minced (about 10 grams)
- 1 tablespoon chopped fresh parsley (about 4 grams)

Directions:

1. Preheat your oven to 200°C (390°F). Line a baking tray with parchment paper.
2. In a large bowl, toss the Brussels sprouts with the olive oil, salt, and pepper. Spread them out evenly on the prepared baking tray.
3. Roast the Brussels sprouts in the preheated oven for 20 minutes, stirring once halfway through.
4. Remove the tray from the oven and sprinkle the grated Parmesan and minced garlic over the Brussels sprouts. Toss to combine.
5. Return the tray to the oven and roast for an additional 5 minutes, or until the cheese is melted and slightly golden.
6. Remove from the oven and sprinkle with chopped parsley before serving.

Nutritional Information: Estimated per serving: 160 calories, 7 grams protein, 8 grams carbohydrates, 12 grams fat, 4 grams fiber, 15 milligrams cholesterol, 410 milligrams sodium, 460 milligrams potassium.

Greek Tzatziki Cucumber Salad

Yield: 4 servings | Prep time: 15 minutes | Cook time: 0 minutes

Ingredients:

- 2 large cucumbers, peeled, deseeded and chopped (about 500 grams)
- 150 grams Greek yogurt, full-fat
- 3 tablespoons extra virgin olive oil (45 ml)
- 2 tablespoons lemon juice (30 ml)
- 2 cloves garlic, minced (about 10 grams)
- 1 tablespoon fresh dill, finely chopped (about 4 grams)
- 1/2 teaspoon salt (2.5 grams)
- 1/4 teaspoon black pepper (0.5 grams)
- 50 grams crumbled feta cheese (optional)
- 50 grams Kalamata olives, pitted and halved (optional)
- 1 small red onion, finely chopped (about 70 grams, optional)

Directions:

1. In a large bowl, combine the chopped cucumbers, Greek yogurt, olive oil, lemon juice, minced garlic, fresh dill, salt, and pepper. Mix well until all the ingredients are well incorporated.
2. Cover the bowl with plastic wrap and refrigerate the salad for at least 30 minutes to allow the flavors to meld together.
3. If desired, add the crumbled feta cheese, Kalamata olives, and finely chopped red onion to the salad. Toss well to combine.
4. Serve the salad cold, as a refreshing side dish or as a light meal on its own.

Nutritional Information: Estimated per serving: 120 calories, 4 grams protein, 7 grams carbohydrates, 9 grams fat, 1 gram fiber, 5 milligrams cholesterol, 320 milligrams sodium, 230 milligrams potassium.

Roasted Garlic Mashed Cauliflower

Yield: 4 servings | Prep time: 10 minutes | Cook time: 40 minutes

Ingredients:

- 1 large head of cauliflower, cut into florets (about 600 grams)
- 1 head of garlic
- 3 tablespoons extra-virgin olive oil (45 ml)
- 50 grams unsalted butter
- 100 ml unsweetened almond milk
- Salt and pepper to taste
- Fresh parsley for garnish (optional)
- 30 grams grated Parmesan cheese (optional)

Directions:

1. Preheat the oven to 200°C (400°F). Slice the top off the head of garlic to expose the cloves, drizzle with 1 tablespoon of olive oil, and wrap in aluminium foil. Place the wrapped garlic in the oven and roast for about 30 minutes, or until the garlic is soft and golden.
2. While the garlic is roasting, bring a large pot of water to a boil. Add the cauliflower florets and cook for about 10 minutes, or until tender. Drain well.
3. In a large bowl, combine the cooked cauliflower, roasted garlic (squeezed out of the skin), butter, remaining olive oil, and almond milk. Use an immersion blender or food processor to blend until smooth and creamy. Season with salt and pepper to taste.
4. Serve the mashed cauliflower in individual bowls, garnished with fresh parsley and grated Parmesan cheese if desired.

Nutritional Information: Estimated per serving: 200 calories, 4 grams protein, 8 grams carbohydrates, 18 grams fat, 3 grams fiber, 25 milligrams cholesterol, 200 milligrams sodium, 400 milligrams potassium.

Zucchini and Parmesan Fritters

Yield: 4 servings | Prep time: 15 minutes | Cook time: 15 minutes

Ingredients:

- 2 medium zucchinis, grated (about 400 grams)
- 1 teaspoon salt (5 grams)
- 2 large eggs
- 80 grams grated Parmesan cheese
- 1 clove garlic, minced
- 1 teaspoon dried oregano (1 gram)
- 1 teaspoon dried basil (1 gram)
- 1/4 teaspoon black pepper (0.5 grams)
- 2 tablespoons coconut oil (30 ml) for frying

Directions:

1. Place the grated zucchini in a colander, sprinkle with salt, and toss to combine. Let it sit for about 10 minutes to draw out excess moisture. Squeeze out the excess moisture with a clean kitchen towel or paper towels.
2. In a mixing bowl, beat the eggs and add the grated Parmesan cheese, minced garlic, dried oregano, dried basil, and black pepper. Mix well. Add the squeezed zucchini to the bowl and mix to combine.
3. Heat the coconut oil in a large non-stick frying pan over medium heat. Once the oil is hot, scoop out tablespoons of the zucchini mixture and drop them into the pan. Flatten each fritter with the back of the spoon. Cook for about 3 minutes on each side or until golden brown and crispy.
4. Remove the fritters from the pan and place them on a plate lined with paper towels to drain any excess oil. Serve hot.

Nutritional Information: Estimated per serving: 150 calories, 8 grams protein, 4 grams carbohydrates, 11 grams fat, 1 gram fiber, 95 milligrams cholesterol, 700 milligrams sodium, 300 milligrams potassium.

Creamy Keto Coleslaw
Yield: 4 servings | Prep time: 15 minutes | Cook time: 0 minutes

Ingredients:

- 400 grams white cabbage, thinly sliced
- 100 grams red cabbage, thinly sliced
- 100 grams carrots, grated
- 2 spring onions, thinly sliced
- 120 ml mayonnaise
- 2 tablespoons apple cider vinegar (30 ml)
- 1 tablespoon Dijon mustard (15 grams)
- 1 tablespoon erythritol or other keto-friendly sweetener (15 grams)
- 1/4 teaspoon salt (1.25 grams)
- 1/4 teaspoon black pepper (0.5 grams)

Directions:

1. In a large mixing bowl, combine the sliced white cabbage, red cabbage, grated carrots, and sliced spring onions.
2. In a separate small bowl, whisk together the mayonnaise, apple cider vinegar, Dijon mustard, erythritol, salt, and black pepper until smooth and well combined.
3. Pour the dressing over the vegetables and toss until everything is evenly coated.
4. Refrigerate the coleslaw for at least 30 minutes before serving to allow the flavours to meld together. Serve chilled.

Nutritional Information: Estimated per serving: 200 calories, 1 gram protein, 6 grams carbohydrates, 18 grams fat, 2 grams fiber, 12 milligrams cholesterol, 320 milligrams sodium, 170 milligrams potassium.

Asparagus and Prosciutto Bundles
Yield: 4 servings | Prep time: 10 minutes | Cook time: 10 minutes

Ingredients:

- 16 asparagus spears (approximately 400 grams)
- 8 slices of prosciutto (approximately 100 grams)
- 2 tablespoons of olive oil (30 ml)
- 1/4 teaspoon of black pepper (0.5 grams)
- 1/4 teaspoon of garlic powder (0.5 grams)
- 50 grams of grated Parmesan cheese

Directions:

1. Preheat your oven to 200°C (390°F) and line a baking sheet with parchment paper.
2. Trim the tough ends of the asparagus spears. Toss the asparagus with olive oil, black pepper, and garlic powder until well coated.
3. Take two asparagus spears and wrap them with one slice of prosciutto. Place the wrapped bundle onto the prepared baking sheet.
4. Repeat with the remaining asparagus and prosciutto until all bundles are formed.
5. Sprinkle the bundles with the grated Parmesan cheese.
6. Roast the bundles in the preheated oven for 10 minutes, or until the asparagus is tender and the prosciutto is crispy.
7. Serve immediately.

Nutritional Information: Estimated per serving: 135 calories, 8 grams protein, 4 grams carbohydrates, 10 grams fat, 2 grams fiber, 20 milligrams cholesterol, 400 milligrams sodium, 245 milligrams potassium.

Keto Italian Antipasto Salad

Yield: 4 servings | Prep time: 20 minutes | Cook time: 0 minutes

Ingredients:

- 200 grams of mixed salad greens (such as romaine, arugula, and spinach)
- 100 grams of cherry tomatoes, halved
- 100 grams of cucumber, sliced
- 50 grams of red onion, thinly sliced
- 100 grams of green olives, pitted
- 100 grams of salami, sliced
- 100 grams of provolone cheese, cubed
- 100 grams of mozzarella cheese, cubed
- 50 grams of roasted red pepper strips
- 50 grams of artichoke hearts, drained and quartered
- 4 tablespoons of extra virgin olive oil (60 ml)
- 2 tablespoons of red wine vinegar (30 ml)
- 1/2 teaspoon of dried oregano (1 gram)
- 1/2 teaspoon of dried basil (1 gram)
- 1/4 teaspoon of garlic powder (0.5 grams)
- Salt and black pepper to taste

Directions:

1. In a large salad bowl, combine the salad greens, cherry tomatoes, cucumber, red onion, green olives, salami, provolone cheese, mozzarella cheese, roasted red pepper strips, and artichoke hearts.
2. In a small bowl, whisk together the olive oil, red wine vinegar, oregano, basil, garlic powder, salt, and black pepper until well combined.
3. Pour the dressing over the salad and toss gently to coat all the ingredients with the dressing.
4. Serve immediately.

Nutritional Information: Estimated per serving: 385 calories, 18 grams protein, 6 grams carbohydrates, 32 grams fat, 2 grams fiber, 45 milligrams cholesterol, 950 milligrams sodium, 380 milligrams potassium.

Lemon Herb Roasted Asparagus

Yield: 4 servings | Prep time: 10 minutes | Cook time: 15 minutes

Ingredients:

- 400 grams of fresh asparagus, tough ends trimmed
- 3 tablespoons of extra virgin olive oil (45 ml)
- Zest and juice of 1 lemon
- 2 garlic cloves, finely minced
- 1 teaspoon of fresh thyme leaves (2 grams)
- 1 teaspoon of fresh rosemary, finely chopped (2 grams)
- Salt and black pepper to taste
- Grated Parmesan cheese for garnish (optional)

Directions:

1. Preheat your oven to 200°C (400°F). Line a baking tray with parchment paper.
2. In a mixing bowl, combine the olive oil, lemon zest, lemon juice, minced garlic, thyme, rosemary, salt, and pepper. Whisk well to combine.
3. Place the asparagus on the prepared baking tray and drizzle with the lemon herb mixture. Toss to coat evenly.
4. Roast the asparagus in the oven for 12-15 minutes or until tender and slightly golden.
5. Serve immediately with a sprinkle of grated Parmesan cheese if desired.

Nutritional Information: Estimated per serving: 85 calories, 2 grams protein, 4 grams carbohydrates, 7 grams fat, 2 grams fiber, 0 milligrams cholesterol, 2 milligrams sodium, 229 milligrams potassium.

Bacon, Cheddar, and Chive Deviled Eggs

Yield: 4 servings | Prep time: 15 minutes | Cook time: 10 minutes

Ingredients:

- 8 large eggs
- 4 rashers of bacon, cooked and crumbled
- 60 grams of cheddar cheese, grated
- 4 tablespoons of mayonnaise (60 grams)
- 1 tablespoon of Dijon mustard (15 grams)
- 1 tablespoon of chives, finely chopped (3 grams)
- Salt and pepper to taste
- Paprika for garnish

Directions:

1. Place the eggs in a single layer in a saucepan. Add enough cold water to cover the eggs. Bring to a boil over high heat. Once boiling, reduce the heat to low, cover, and simmer for 10 minutes. Remove from heat and transfer the eggs to an ice-water bath to cool.
2. Once cooled, peel the eggs and cut them in half lengthwise. Remove the yolks and place them in a bowl. Set the egg whites aside.
3. Mash the yolks with a fork. Add the mayonnaise, mustard, cheddar cheese, bacon, chives, salt, and pepper. Mix until well combined.
4. Spoon the yolk mixture into the egg whites. Garnish with paprika and additional chives if desired.
5. Serve immediately or refrigerate until ready to serve.

Nutritional Information: Estimated per serving: 250 calories, 13 grams protein, 2 grams carbohydrates, 21 grams fat, 0 grams fiber, 210 milligrams cholesterol, 420 milligrams sodium, 130 milligrams potassium.

Loaded Keto Cauliflower Casserole

Yield: 4 servings | Prep time: 15 minutes | Cook time: 30 minutes

Ingredients:

- 1 large head of cauliflower (600 grams), cut into florets
- 150 grams of sour cream
- 100 grams of cheddar cheese, grated
- 100 grams of mozzarella cheese, grated
- 4 rashers of bacon, cooked and crumbled
- 3 green onions, chopped (30 grams)
- 2 cloves of garlic, minced (6 grams)
- Salt and pepper to taste

Directions:

1. Preheat your oven to 200°C (400°F).
2. Steam the cauliflower florets until tender, about 8-10 minutes. Drain well and transfer to a large mixing bowl.
3. Add the sour cream, half of the cheddar cheese, half of the mozzarella cheese, half of the bacon, green onions, garlic, salt, and pepper to the cauliflower. Mix well.
4. Transfer the mixture to a greased baking dish. Top with the remaining cheddar and mozzarella cheese.
5. Bake in the preheated oven for 15-20 minutes, until the cheese is melted and bubbly.
6. Garnish with the remaining bacon and serve.

Nutritional Information: Estimated per serving: 345 calories, 16 grams protein, 10 grams carbohydrates, 27 grams fat, 3 grams fiber, 75 milligrams cholesterol, 510 milligrams sodium, 400 milligrams potassium.

Avocado and Bacon Spinach Salad

Yield: 4 servings | Prep time: 10 minutes | Cook time: 10 minutes

Ingredients:

- 200 grams of baby spinach
- 2 ripe avocados, pitted, peeled, and sliced
- 8 rashers of bacon
- 50 grams of feta cheese, crumbled
- 1 small red onion, thinly sliced (70 grams)
- 2 tablespoons of extra-virgin olive oil (30 mL)
- 2 tablespoons of apple cider vinegar (30 mL)
- 1 teaspoon of Dijon mustard (5 grams)
- Salt and pepper, to taste

Directions:

1. In a large frying pan, cook the bacon over medium heat until crisp. Remove from the pan and let it cool on a paper towel. Once cooled, crumble the bacon into small pieces.
2. In a small bowl, whisk together the olive oil, apple cider vinegar, Dijon mustard, salt, and pepper until well combined.
3. In a large salad bowl, combine the baby spinach, sliced avocados, crumbled bacon, feta cheese, and red onion. Toss gently to mix.
4. Drizzle the dressing over the salad and toss gently to coat all the ingredients with the dressing.
5. Serve immediately.

Nutritional Information: Estimated per serving: 390 calories, 12 grams protein, 11 grams carbohydrates, 35 grams fat, 7 grams fiber, 30 milligrams cholesterol, 510 milligrams sodium, 730 milligrams potassium.

Cheesy Keto Garlic Breadsticks

Yield: 4 servings | Prep time: 15 minutes | Cook time: 15 minutes

Ingredients:

- 170 grams of mozzarella cheese, shredded
- 85 grams of almond flour
- 2 tablespoons of cream cheese (30 grams)
- 1 large egg
- 1 teaspoon of baking powder (5 grams)
- 1/2 teaspoon of garlic powder (2.5 grams)
- 1/4 teaspoon of salt (1.25 grams)
- 1/4 teaspoon of black pepper (0.5 grams)
- 50 grams of cheddar cheese, shredded
- 2 tablespoons of unsalted butter (30 grams)
- 2 cloves of garlic, minced (6 grams)
- 1 tablespoon of chopped fresh parsley (4 grams)

Directions:

1. Preheat your oven to 200°C (390°F) and line a baking sheet with parchment paper.
2. In a microwave-safe bowl, combine the mozzarella and cream cheese. Microwave on high for 1 minute, then stir and microwave for another 30 seconds, or until the cheeses are fully melted and combined.
3. Stir in the almond flour, egg, baking powder, garlic powder, salt, and pepper. Knead the dough until well combined.
4. Spread the dough onto the prepared baking sheet in a rectangle shape, about 1 cm thick. Sprinkle with the cheddar cheese.
5. Bake for 12-15 minutes or until the edges are golden brown.
6. In a small saucepan, melt the butter over medium heat. Add the garlic and cook for 1 minute. Remove from the heat and stir in the parsley. Brush the garlic butter mixture over the breadsticks.
7. Slice the breadsticks and serve immediately.

Nutritional Information: Estimated per serving: 325 calories, 16 grams protein, 6 grams carbohydrates, 27 grams fat, 3 grams fiber, 85 milligrams cholesterol, 560 milligrams sodium, 180 milligrams potassium.

Creamy Cucumber Dill Salad

Yield: 4 servings | Prep time: 10 minutes | Cook time: 0 minutes

Ingredients:

- 2 large cucumbers (about 400 grams), thinly sliced
- 1 small red onion (about 70 grams), thinly sliced
- 120 grams of full-fat Greek yogurt
- 2 tablespoons of fresh dill, chopped (8 grams)
- 1 tablespoon of apple cider vinegar (15 millilitres)
- 1 teaspoon of olive oil (5 millilitres)
- 1 clove of garlic, minced (3 grams)
- 1/2 teaspoon of salt (2.5 grams)
- 1/4 teaspoon of black pepper (0.5 grams)

Directions:

1. In a large bowl, combine the cucumber slices and red onion slices.
2. In a separate bowl, whisk together the Greek yogurt, dill, apple cider vinegar, olive oil, garlic, salt, and pepper until smooth and creamy.
3. Pour the dressing over the cucumber and onion mixture. Toss gently to coat the vegetables in the dressing.
4. Refrigerate for at least 30 minutes before serving to allow the flavors to meld.
5. Serve chilled and enjoy!

Nutritional Information: Estimated per serving: 70 calories, 4 grams protein, 8 grams carbohydrates, 3 grams fat, 1 gram fiber, 2 milligrams cholesterol, 320 milligrams sodium, 230 milligrams potassium.

Keto Comfort Foods: British Classics Reimagined

Keto Cottage Pie

Yield: 4 servings | Prep time: 15 minutes | Cook time: 45 minutes

Ingredients:

- 450 grams of ground beef
- 1 medium onion (about 150 grams), chopped
- 2 cloves garlic (about 6 grams), minced
- 2 tablespoons (30 millilitres) of olive oil
- 1 medium carrot (about 60 grams), diced
- 100 grams of mushrooms, chopped
- 2 tablespoons (30 millilitres) of tomato paste
- 240 millilitres of beef broth
- 1/2 teaspoon (2.5 grams) of dried thyme

- 1/2 teaspoon (2.5 grams) of dried rosemary
- Salt and pepper, to taste
-
- For the topping:
- 500 grams of cauliflower florets
- 30 grams of butter
- 50 grams of cheddar cheese, shredded
- Salt and pepper, to taste

Directions:

1. Preheat your oven to 200°C (392°F).
2. In a large pan, heat the olive oil over medium heat. Add the onions and garlic, and sauté until the onions are translucent. Add the ground beef and cook until browned. Drain any excess fat.
3. Add the carrots, mushrooms, tomato paste, beef broth, thyme, rosemary, salt, and pepper. Simmer for about 10 minutes until the vegetables are tender and the sauce thickens.
4. Transfer the meat mixture to a baking dish and spread it out evenly.
5. For the topping, steam the cauliflower florets until tender. Mash the cauliflower with the butter, cheddar cheese, salt, and pepper until smooth.
6. Spread the mashed cauliflower over the meat mixture in the baking dish.
7. Bake for 25-30 minutes or until the top is golden brown and the edges are bubbling.
8. Let the cottage pie cool for a few minutes before serving.

Nutritional Information: Estimated per serving: 530 calories, 30 grams protein, 15 grams carbohydrates, 40 grams fat, 4 grams fiber, 120 milligrams cholesterol, 700 milligrams sodium, 800 milligrams potassium.

Keto Yorkshire Puddings

Yield: 6 servings | Prep time: 10 minutes | Cook time: 25 minutes

Ingredients:

- 4 large eggs (about 220 grams)
- 100 millilitres of almond milk
- 1/2 teaspoon (2.5 grams) of xanthan gum
- 50 grams of coconut flour

- 50 grams of almond flour
- 1/4 teaspoon (1.25 grams) of salt
- 70 millilitres of beef dripping or vegetable oil

Directions:

1. Preheat your oven to 220°C (428°F). Place a little of the beef dripping or vegetable oil into each of the compartments of a 12-hole muffin tin, and place the tin in the oven to heat up while you prepare the batter.
2. In a medium-sized bowl, whisk together the eggs and almond milk until well combined.
3. In a separate bowl, combine the coconut flour, almond flour, xanthan gum, and salt. Gradually add the dry ingredients to the wet ingredients, whisking continuously until you have a smooth batter.
4. Carefully remove the hot muffin tin from the oven. Pour the batter into the compartments of the muffin tin, filling each one about halfway.
5. Return the muffin tin to the oven and bake for 20-25 minutes, or until the puddings have risen and are golden brown.
6. Serve immediately with roast beef and gravy, or any other main dish of your choice.

Nutritional Information: Estimated per serving: 145 calories, 6 grams protein, 5 grams carbohydrates, 11 grams fat, 3 grams fiber, 120 milligrams cholesterol, 140 milligrams sodium, 85 milligrams potassium.

Cauliflower Cheese Soup

Yield: 4 servings | Prep time: 10 minutes | Cook time: 25 minutes

Ingredients:

- 1 medium cauliflower (about 600 grams), cut into florets
- 1 medium onion (about 150 grams), chopped
- 2 cloves garlic (about 6 grams), minced
- 2 tablespoons (30 millilitres) of olive oil
- 750 millilitres of chicken or vegetable broth
- 200 millilitres of heavy cream
- 200 grams of cheddar cheese, shredded
- 1 teaspoon (5 grams) of salt
- 1/2 teaspoon (2.5 grams) of black pepper
- 1/2 teaspoon (2.5 grams) of paprika
- Fresh parsley, for garnish

Directions:

1. In a large pot, heat the olive oil over medium heat. Add the onions and garlic, and sauté until the onions are translucent.
2. Add the cauliflower florets and broth to the pot. Bring the mixture to a boil, then reduce the heat to low and simmer for about 15 minutes or until the cauliflower is tender.
3. Use an immersion blender or a regular blender to puree the soup until smooth. If using a regular blender, be careful when blending hot liquids and blend in batches if necessary.
4. Return the soup to the pot and heat over low heat. Stir in the heavy cream, cheddar cheese, salt, pepper, and paprika. Cook until the cheese is melted and the soup is heated through.
5. Serve the soup in bowls and garnish with fresh parsley.

Nutritional Information: Estimated per serving: 410 calories, 17 grams protein, 13 grams carbohydrates, 34 grams fat, 4 grams fiber, 90 milligrams cholesterol, 1000 milligrams sodium, 600 milligrams potassium.

Keto Bangers and Mash

Yield: 4 servings | Prep time: 15 minutes | Cook time: 30 minutes

Ingredients:

For the bangers:
- 8 sausages (about 500 grams), preferably high-quality pork or beef sausages
- 1 tablespoon (15 millilitres) of olive oil

For the mash:
- 1 large cauliflower head (about 600 grams), cut into florets
- 50 grams of butter
- 100 grams of cream cheese

- Salt and pepper to taste

For the gravy:
- 1 small onion (about 70 grams), finely chopped
- 1 tablespoon (15 millilitres) of olive oil
- 250 millilitres of beef broth
- 1 teaspoon (5 grams) of xanthan gum
- Salt and pepper to taste

Directions:

1. Heat the olive oil in a large frying pan over medium-high heat. Add the sausages and cook until browned on all sides and cooked through, about 10-15 minutes. Remove the sausages from the pan and set aside.
2. In the same pan, add the onion for the gravy and sauté until softened, about 5 minutes. Add the beef broth and bring to a simmer. Sprinkle the xanthan gum over the broth and whisk until the gravy thickens. Season with salt and pepper to taste.
3. While the sausages and gravy are cooking, steam the cauliflower florets until tender, about 8-10 minutes. Drain and transfer the cauliflower to a food processor.
4. Add the butter and cream cheese to the food processor with the cauliflower. Process until smooth. Season with salt and pepper to taste.
5. Serve the sausages over the cauliflower mash and top with the gravy.

Nutritional Information: Estimated per serving: 620 calories, 28 grams protein, 9 grams carbohydrates, 51 grams fat, 5 grams fiber, 120 milligrams cholesterol, 1,300 milligrams sodium, 700 milligrams potassium.

Keto Beef and Ale Stew

Yield: 6 servings | Prep time: 15 minutes | Cook time: 180 minutes

Ingredients:

- 1 kg of beef stew meat, cut into chunks
- 1 tablespoon (15 millilitres) of olive oil
- 1 large onion (about 150 grams), chopped
- 3 cloves of garlic (about 9 grams), minced
- 300 millilitres of dark ale (low carb)
- 500 millilitres of beef broth
- 2 bay leaves
- 1 teaspoon (5 grams) of dried thyme
- 1 teaspoon (5 grams) of dried rosemary
- 2 medium turnips (about 300 grams), peeled and chopped
- 200 grams of mushrooms, sliced
- Salt and pepper to taste
- 2 tablespoons (30 grams) of xanthan gum (optional, for thickening)

Directions:

1. In a large pot, heat the olive oil over medium-high heat. Add the beef and brown on all sides, about 5-7 minutes. Remove the beef and set aside.
2. In the same pot, add the onion and garlic and sauté until softened, about 3-5 minutes. Add the beef back into the pot along with the ale, beef broth, bay leaves, thyme, rosemary, and a pinch of salt and pepper.
3. Bring the mixture to a boil, then reduce the heat to low and simmer, covered, for 2 hours, stirring occasionally.
4. Add the turnips and mushrooms to the pot and continue to simmer, uncovered, for another 30-45 minutes, until the vegetables are tender.
5. If desired, thicken the stew by whisking in the xanthan gum until the stew reaches your preferred consistency.
6. Remove the bay leaves and season with additional salt and pepper to taste. Serve hot.

Nutritional Information: Estimated per serving: 350 calories, 40 grams protein, 12 grams carbohydrates, 15 grams fat, 3 grams fiber, 120 milligrams cholesterol, 800 milligrams sodium, 900 milligrams potassium.

Keto Toad in the Hole

Yield: 4 servings | Prep time: 15 minutes | Cook time: 35 minutes

Ingredients:

- 6 keto-friendly sausages (about 400 grams)
- 4 large eggs (about 220 grams)
- 120 millilitres of almond milk
- 1/2 teaspoon (2.5 grams) of xanthan gum
- 70 grams of coconut flour
- 70 grams of almond flour
- 1/4 teaspoon (1.25 grams) of salt
- 70 millilitres of beef dripping or vegetable oil

Directions:

1. Preheat your oven to 220°C (428°F). Place the beef dripping or vegetable oil into a large ovenproof dish and place it in the oven to heat up while you prepare the batter and sausages.
2. In a medium-sized bowl, whisk together the eggs and almond milk until well combined.
3. In a separate bowl, combine the coconut flour, almond flour, xanthan gum, and salt. Gradually add the dry ingredients to the wet ingredients, whisking continuously until you have a smooth batter. Set the batter aside.
4. In a frying pan, cook the keto-friendly sausages until they are browned on all sides but not fully cooked through.
5. Carefully remove the hot ovenproof dish from the oven. Place the sausages in the dish, then pour the batter over them.
6. Return the dish to the oven and bake for 30-35 minutes, or until the batter has risen and is golden brown. Serve immediately with keto-friendly gravy and vegetables of your choice.

Nutritional Information: Estimated per serving: 575 calories, 26 grams protein, 8 grams carbohydrates, 49 grams fat, 5 grams fiber, 230 milligrams cholesterol, 950 milligrams sodium, 370 milligrams potassium.

Cauliflower Shepherd's Pie

Yield: 6 servings | Prep time: 15 minutes | Cook time: 45 minutes

Ingredients:

- 1 kg of ground beef or lamb
- 1 medium onion (about 150 grams), chopped
- 2 cloves of garlic (about 6 grams), minced
- 1 medium carrot (about 60 grams), chopped
- 2 stalks of celery (about 80 grams), chopped
- 400 grams of cauliflower florets
- 4 tablespoons (60 millilitres) of heavy cream

- 2 tablespoons (30 grams) of butter
- 1 tablespoon (15 millilitres) of olive oil
- 1 tablespoon (15 grams) of tomato paste
- 1 teaspoon (5 grams) of dried rosemary
- 1 teaspoon (5 grams) of dried thyme
- Salt and pepper to taste
- 200 grams of grated cheddar cheese

Directions:

1. Preheat the oven to 200°C (400°F).
2. In a large frying pan, heat the olive oil over medium-high heat. Add the ground meat, onion, garlic, carrot, and celery. Cook, breaking up the meat, until browned and the vegetables are softened, about 8-10 minutes. Stir in the tomato paste, rosemary, thyme, and season with salt and pepper to taste.
3. Transfer the meat mixture to a baking dish and spread it out evenly.
4. In a pot of boiling water, cook the cauliflower florets until tender, about 5-7 minutes. Drain the cauliflower and transfer to a blender or food processor. Add the heavy cream, butter, and a pinch of salt and pepper. Blend until smooth.
5. Spread the cauliflower mash over the meat mixture in the baking dish. Sprinkle the grated cheddar cheese on top.
6. Bake in the preheated oven for 25-30 minutes, until the top is golden brown and bubbly. Let the pie cool for a few minutes before serving.

Nutritional Information: Estimated per serving: 450 calories, 30 grams protein, 10 grams carbohydrates, 33 grams fat, 3 grams fiber, 100 milligrams cholesterol, 500 milligrams sodium, 500 milligrams potassium.

Keto Bubble and Squeak

Yield: 4 servings | Prep time: 15 minutes | Cook time: 20 minutes

Ingredients:

- 400 grams of cauliflower florets
- 200 grams of savoy cabbage, finely shredded
- 4 rashers of bacon, diced
- 2 medium leeks, thinly sliced
- 2 tablespoons of butter

- 1 tablespoon of olive oil
- 1/2 teaspoon of salt
- 1/4 teaspoon of black pepper
- 1 teaspoon of fresh parsley, chopped (optional)

Directions:

1. Bring a large pot of salted water to a boil. Add the cauliflower florets and cook for 6-8 minutes, or until tender. Drain well and transfer to a large mixing bowl. Mash with a fork or potato masher until smooth.
2. In a large skillet over medium heat, cook the bacon until crispy. Remove and set aside. In the same skillet, add the butter and leeks. Cook for 4-5 minutes, or until the leeks are softened.
3. Add the shredded cabbage to the skillet and cook for another 5-7 minutes, or until wilted and tender. Season with salt and pepper.
4. Stir the cabbage and leek mixture into the mashed cauliflower. Add the crispy bacon and mix well.
5. In a clean skillet, heat the olive oil over medium-high heat. Add the cauliflower mixture and press down firmly with a spatula. Cook for 5-7 minutes, or until the bottom is golden and crispy.
6. Flip the bubble and squeak over and cook for another 5-7 minutes, or until the other side is golden and crispy. Serve hot, garnished with fresh parsley if desired.

Nutritional Information: Estimated per serving: 180 calories, 6 grams protein, 8 grams carbohydrates, 14 grams fat, 4 grams fiber, 25 milligrams cholesterol, 500 milligrams sodium, 450 milligrams potassium.

Keto Ploughman's Lunch

Yield: 4 servings | Prep time: 15 minutes | Cook time: 0 minutes

Ingredients:

- 240 grams of Cheddar cheese, sliced
- 240 grams of cooked ham or turkey, sliced
- 100 grams of cherry tomatoes, halved
- 60 grams of cucumber, sliced
- 60 grams of radishes, sliced
- 80 grams of pickled onions
- 60 grams of pickled gherkins
- 40 grams of whole grain mustard
- 120 grams of hard-boiled eggs, peeled and halved
- 80 grams of mixed salad greens
- 40 grams of celery, sliced
- 40 grams of walnuts
- 80 grams of keto-friendly pork scratchings

Directions:

1. Arrange the cheese and ham or turkey slices on a large serving platter.
2. Add the cherry tomatoes, cucumber, radishes, pickled onions, and pickled gherkins to the platter.
3. Place a small bowl of whole grain mustard in the center of the platter.
4. Add the hard-boiled eggs, mixed salad greens, celery, and walnuts to the platter.
5. Serve with a bowl of pork scratchings on the side.

Nutritional Information: Estimated per serving: 505 calories, 32 grams protein, 8 grams carbohydrates, 38 grams fat, 3 grams fiber, 200 milligrams cholesterol, 1070 milligrams sodium, 400 milligrams potassium.

Keto Chicken Tikka Masala

Yield: 4 servings | Prep time: 15 minutes | Cook time: 30 minutes

Ingredients:

- 500 grams of boneless, skinless chicken thighs, cut into bite-sized pieces
- 1 large onion (about 150 grams), finely chopped
- 3 cloves of garlic (about 9 grams), minced
- 1 tablespoon (15 grams) of ginger, minced
- 1 tablespoon (15 grams) of ghee or butter
- 1 tablespoon (15 millilitres) of olive oil
- 2 teaspoons (10 grams) of garam masala
- 1 teaspoon (5 grams) of turmeric
- 1 teaspoon (5 grams) of cumin
- 1 teaspoon (5 grams) of paprika
- 1 teaspoon (5 grams) of ground coriander
- 1/2 teaspoon (2.5 grams) of chili powder (adjust to taste)
- 400 grams of canned tomatoes, crushed
- 200 millilitres of heavy cream
- Salt and pepper to taste
- Fresh coriander leaves for garnish

Directions:

1. In a large frying pan, heat the ghee or butter and olive oil over medium-high heat. Add the onion, garlic, and ginger. Cook, stirring occasionally, until the onions are soft and translucent, about 5-7 minutes.
2. Add the chicken to the pan and cook until browned on all sides, about 5-7 minutes.
3. Add the garam masala, turmeric, cumin, paprika, ground coriander, chili powder, salt, and pepper to the pan. Stir well to coat the chicken with the spices.
4. Add the crushed tomatoes to the pan and stir to combine. Bring the mixture to a simmer, reduce the heat to low, and cover the pan. Cook for 15-20 minutes, stirring occasionally, until the chicken is cooked through and the sauce has thickened.
5. Stir in the heavy cream and cook for an additional 2-3 minutes, until heated through.
6. Serve the chicken tikka masala over cauliflower rice or with low-carb naan bread. Garnish with fresh coriander leaves.

Nutritional Information: Estimated per serving: 390 calories, 25 grams protein, 10 grams carbohydrates, 28 grams fat, 2 grams fiber, 120 milligrams cholesterol, 350 milligrams sodium, 500 milligrams potassium.

Keto Eton Mess

Yield: 4 servings | Prep time: 15 minutes | Cook time: 0 minutes

Ingredients:

- 300 grams of fresh strawberries, hulled and halved
- 240 ml of double cream
- 4 large egg whites
- 100 grams of erythritol (or other keto-friendly sweetener)
- 1 teaspoon of vanilla extract
- Optional: Fresh mint leaves for garnish

Directions:

1. In a large mixing bowl, beat the egg whites until soft peaks form. Gradually add the erythritol while continuing to beat until stiff peaks form.
2. In a separate bowl, whip the double cream with the vanilla extract until thickened.
3. Gently fold the whipped cream into the beaten egg whites until just combined.
4. In individual serving dishes, layer the meringue mixture with the strawberries. Repeat the layers until all the ingredients are used up.
5. Garnish with fresh mint leaves if desired.
6. Serve immediately, or refrigerate until ready to serve.

Nutritional Information: Estimated per serving: 320 calories, 4 grams protein, 8 grams carbohydrates, 30 grams fat, 2 grams fiber, 100 milligrams cholesterol, 50 milligrams sodium, 180 milligrams potassium.

Keto Cornish Pasties

Yield: 6 servings | Prep time: 25 minutes | Cook time: 35 minutes

Ingredients:

For the Pastry:
- 200 grams of almond flour
- 50 grams of coconut flour
- 1 teaspoon of xanthan gum
- 1/2 teaspoon of salt
- 1/2 teaspoon of baking powder
- 100 grams of butter, chilled and cubed
- 2 large eggs

For the Filling:
- 300 grams of beef skirt steak or chuck steak, diced
- 150 grams of turnips or swede, diced
- 1 medium onion, finely chopped
- 1 tablespoon of olive oil
- 1/2 teaspoon of salt
- 1/4 teaspoon of black pepper
- 1/2 teaspoon of dried thyme

Directions:

1. In a large bowl, combine the almond flour, coconut flour, xanthan gum, salt, and baking powder. Add the chilled butter and use a pastry blender or your fingers to cut the butter into the flour mixture until it resembles coarse crumbs.
2. Add the eggs to the bowl and mix until a dough forms. Knead the dough a few times, then wrap it in plastic wrap and refrigerate for 15 minutes.
3. Preheat your oven to 180°C (350°F).
4. In a large skillet, heat the olive oil over medium heat. Add the onion and cook for 2-3 minutes, or until softened. Add the beef and cook for 4-5 minutes, or until browned. Add the turnips, salt, pepper, and thyme, and cook for another 5 minutes, or until the turnips are tender.
5. Roll out the chilled dough between two sheets of parchment paper to a thickness of 5 mm. Cut out 6 circles, each about 15 cm in diameter.
6. Divide the filling evenly among the circles, leaving a border of about 2 cm. Fold the dough over the filling to form a half-moon shape and crimp the edges to seal.
7. Place the pasties on a baking sheet lined with parchment paper and bake for 25-30 minutes, or until golden brown. Serve hot.

Nutritional Information: Estimated per serving: 440 calories, 22 grams protein, 12 grams carbohydrates, 36 grams fat, 5 grams fiber, 120 milligrams cholesterol, 550 milligrams sodium, 350 milligrams potassium.

Keto Full English Breakfast

Yield: 4 servings | Prep time: 10 minutes | Cook time: 20 minutes

Ingredients:

- 4 large eggs
- 8 rashers of bacon
- 4 pork sausages (check for low-carb, high-fat options)
- 200 grams of mushrooms, sliced
- 150 grams of cherry tomatoes, halved
- 1 medium avocado, sliced
- 50 grams of butter
- Salt and pepper to taste
- Optional: Fresh parsley for garnish

Directions:

1. Heat a large frying pan over medium-high heat. Add the bacon and sausages and cook until browned and cooked through, about 8-10 minutes. Remove from the pan and set aside.
2. In the same pan, add half of the butter and add the mushrooms. Cook for 5-6 minutes, or until browned and tender. Remove from the pan and set aside.
3. In the same pan, add the remaining butter and add the cherry tomatoes. Cook for 2-3 minutes, or until slightly softened. Season with salt and pepper. Remove from the pan and set aside.
4. In the same pan, crack the eggs and fry them to your liking. Season with salt and pepper.
5. Serve the eggs, bacon, sausages, mushrooms, tomatoes, and avocado slices on a plate. Garnish with fresh parsley if desired.

Nutritional Information: Estimated per serving: 520 calories, 25 grams protein, 8 grams carbohydrates, 44 grams fat, 5 grams fiber, 250 milligrams cholesterol, 1100 milligrams sodium, 650 milligrams potassium.

Keto Steak and Kidney Pie

Yield: 6 servings | Prep time: 25 minutes | Cook time: 2 hours 30 minutes

Ingredients:

- 700 grams of beef stewing steak, diced
- 200 grams of beef kidney, diced
- 70 grams of coconut flour
- 2 tablespoons of olive oil
- 1 large onion, diced
- 3 cloves of garlic, minced
- 1 teaspoon of salt
- 1/2 teaspoon of black pepper
- 500 milliliters of beef broth
- 2 tablespoons of tomato paste
- 1 tablespoon of Worcestershire sauce
- 2 bay leaves
- 1 teaspoon of dried thyme

For the crust:
- 180 grams of almond flour
- 60 grams of coconut flour
- 1/2 teaspoon of salt
- 110 grams of cold butter, cubed
- 1 large egg

Directions:

1. In a large bowl, toss the diced steak and kidney with the coconut flour until well-coated.
2. In a large, oven-proof skillet or casserole dish, heat the olive oil over medium-high heat. Add the onion and garlic, and cook for 2-3 minutes until softened.
3. Add the floured meat to the skillet and brown on all sides. Season with salt and pepper.
4. Stir in the beef broth, tomato paste, Worcestershire sauce, bay leaves, and thyme. Bring to a simmer.
5. Cover and place in a preheated oven at 160°C for 2 hours, stirring occasionally.
6. While the meat is cooking, prepare the crust. In a food processor, pulse the almond flour, coconut flour, salt, and cold butter until the mixture resembles breadcrumbs.
7. Add the egg and pulse until a dough forms. Wrap in plastic wrap and chill in the fridge for 30 minutes.
8. Once the meat has finished cooking, remove from the oven and increase the temperature to 190°C. Discard the bay leaves.
9. Roll out the chilled dough between two sheets of parchment paper to fit the top of your skillet or casserole dish. Place the dough on top of the meat mixture and press down around the edges to seal. Make a few small slits in the top to allow steam to escape. Bake for 25-30 minutes, or until the crust is golden brown.

Nutritional Information: Estimated per serving: 540 calories, 34 grams protein, 20 grams carbohydrates, 35 grams fat, 6 grams fiber, 145 milligrams cholesterol, 900 milligrams sodium, 550 milligrams potassium.

Keto Fish and Chips with Tartar Sauce

Yield: 4 servings | Prep time: 15 minutes | Cook time: 20 minutes

Ingredients:

For the fish:
- 4 white fish fillets (about 600 grams), such as cod or haddock
- 80 grams of almond flour
- 1 tablespoon (15 grams) of coconut flour
- 1 teaspoon (5 grams) of paprika
- 1 teaspoon (5 grams) of garlic powder
- 1/2 teaspoon (2.5 grams) of salt
- 1/2 teaspoon (2.5 grams) of black pepper
- 2 large eggs (about 100 grams)
- 4 tablespoons (60 millilitres) of olive oil

For the chips:
- 400 grams of celeriac, peeled and cut into chips

- 2 tablespoons (30 millilitres) of olive oil
- 1 teaspoon (5 grams) of salt
- 1/2 teaspoon (2.5 grams) of black pepper

For the tartar sauce:
- 150 grams of mayonnaise
- 2 tablespoons (30 grams) of dill pickles, finely chopped
- 1 tablespoon (15 grams) of capers, finely chopped
- 1 tablespoon (15 millilitres) of lemon juice
- 1 teaspoon (5 grams) of Dijon mustard
- Salt and pepper to taste

Directions:

1. Preheat the oven to 220°C (425°F). Line a baking sheet with parchment paper.
2. In a shallow bowl, mix together the almond flour, coconut flour, paprika, garlic powder, salt, and pepper. In another bowl, whisk the eggs.
3. Dip each fish fillet into the egg mixture, then coat with the almond flour mixture. Place the fillets on the prepared baking sheet.
4. Toss the celeriac chips with olive oil, salt, and pepper. Spread them out on the baking sheet alongside the fish.
5. Bake in the preheated oven for 15-20 minutes, or until the fish is cooked through and the chips are golden brown.
6. While the fish and chips are baking, mix together all the ingredients for the tartar sauce in a small bowl. Season with salt and pepper to taste.
7. Serve the fish and chips hot with the tartar sauce on the side.

Nutritional Information: Estimated per serving: 540 calories, 36 grams protein, 13 grams carbohydrates, 40 grams fat, 6 grams fiber, 150 milligrams cholesterol, 1,300 milligrams sodium, 700 milligrams potassium.

Desserts for the Sweet-Toothed Keto Enthusiast
Chocolate Avocado Mousse
Yield: 4 servings | Prep time: 10 minutes | Cook time: 0 minutes

Ingredients:

- 2 ripe avocados, peeled and pitted
- 60 grams unsweetened cocoa powder
- 120 millilitres coconut milk
- 80 grams erythritol (or other keto-friendly sweetener)
- 1 teaspoon vanilla extract
- Pinch of salt
- Optional toppings: Shredded coconut, crushed nuts, or fresh berries

Directions:

1. In a blender or food processor, combine the avocados, cocoa powder, coconut milk, erythritol, vanilla extract, and salt. Blend until smooth and creamy.
2. Taste the mousse and adjust the sweetness by adding more erythritol if needed. Blend again to combine.
3. Divide the mousse among four individual serving dishes.
4. Optional: Top with shredded coconut, crushed nuts, or fresh berries as desired.
5. Chill in the refrigerator for at least 1 hour before serving.

Nutritional Information: Estimated per serving: 230 calories, 4 grams protein, 12 grams carbohydrates, 21 grams fat, 8 grams fiber, 0 milligrams cholesterol, 15 milligrams sodium, 480 milligrams potassium.

Raspberry Keto Cheesecake
Yield: 6 servings | Prep time: 15 minutes | Cook time: 60 minutes

Ingredients:

For the crust:
- 100 grams almond flour
- 45 grams melted butter
- 15 grams erythritol (or other keto-friendly sweetener)
- Pinch of salt

For the filling:
- 450 grams cream cheese, softened
- 100 grams erythritol (or other keto-friendly sweetener)
- 2 large eggs
- 1 teaspoon vanilla extract
- 120 millilitres heavy cream

For the topping:
- 150 grams fresh raspberries
- 10 grams erythritol (or other keto-friendly sweetener)

Directions:

1. Preheat the oven to 160°C (320°F). Line the bottom of a 20 cm (8-inch) springform pan with parchment paper.
2. In a medium bowl, mix together the almond flour, melted butter, erythritol, and salt for the crust. Press the mixture into the bottom of the prepared pan. Bake for 10 minutes, then remove from the oven and set aside.
3. In a large bowl, beat the cream cheese with an electric mixer until smooth. Add the erythritol and continue to beat until combined. Beat in the eggs one at a time, followed by the vanilla extract and heavy cream. Pour the filling over the crust in the pan.
4. Bake the cheesecake for 50 minutes, or until the edges are lightly golden and the center is set. Turn off the oven and leave the cheesecake in the oven for an additional 30 minutes. Remove and let it cool to room temperature, then refrigerate for at least 4 hours or overnight.
5. For the topping, mix together the raspberries and erythritol in a small bowl. Spoon the raspberry topping over the cheesecake just before serving.

Nutritional Information: Estimated per serving: 450 calories, 10 grams protein, 8 grams carbohydrates, 42 grams fat, 3 grams fiber, 150 milligrams cholesterol, 280 milligrams sodium, 150 milligrams potassium.

Keto Lemon Curd Tart

Yield: 6 servings | Prep time: 20 minutes | Cook time: 25 minutes

Ingredients:

For the crust:
- 150 grams almond flour
- 45 grams melted butter
- 15 grams erythritol (or other keto-friendly sweetener)
- Pinch of salt

For the lemon curd filling:
- Zest and juice of 2 lemons
- 100 grams erythritol (or other keto-friendly sweetener)
- 60 grams butter
- 3 large egg yolks
- 1 whole large egg

For the topping:
- 120 millilitres double cream, whipped
- Lemon zest for garnish

Directions:

1. Preheat the oven to 180°C (350°F). In a medium bowl, mix together the almond flour, melted butter, erythritol, and salt for the crust. Press the mixture into the bottom and up the sides of a 20 cm (8-inch) tart pan. Bake for 10 minutes, then remove from the oven and set aside.
2. In a small saucepan, combine the lemon zest, juice, erythritol, and butter. Cook over low heat until the butter is melted. In a small bowl, whisk together the egg yolks and whole egg. Gradually whisk the lemon mixture into the eggs to temper them.
3. Return the mixture to the saucepan and cook over low heat, whisking constantly, until the mixture thickens, about 5 minutes. Pour the lemon curd into the prepared crust.
4. Refrigerate the tart for at least 3 hours, until set. Before serving, top with whipped double cream and garnish with lemon zest.

Nutritional Information: Estimated per serving: 370 calories, 9 grams protein, 7 grams carbohydrates, 35 grams fat, 3 grams fiber, 180 milligrams cholesterol, 180 milligrams sodium, 100 milligrams potassium.

Keto Chocolate Chip Cookies

Yield: 12 servings | Prep time: 10 minutes | Cook time: 12 minutes

Ingredients:

- 200 grams almond flour
- 1/2 teaspoon baking powder
- Pinch of salt
- 100 grams butter, softened
- 50 grams erythritol (or other keto-friendly sweetener)
- 1 large egg
- 1 teaspoon vanilla extract
- 100 grams sugar-free chocolate chips

Directions:

1. Preheat the oven to 180°C (350°F). Line a baking sheet with parchment paper.
2. In a medium bowl, whisk together the almond flour, baking powder, and salt.
3. In a large bowl, cream together the butter and erythritol until light and fluffy. Beat in the egg and vanilla extract.
4. Gradually mix the dry ingredients into the wet ingredients until well combined. Fold in the chocolate chips.
5. Drop tablespoons of dough onto the prepared baking sheet. Flatten each cookie slightly with the back of a spoon.
6. Bake for 10-12 minutes, until the edges are golden brown. Let the cookies cool on the baking sheet for 5 minutes, then transfer to a wire rack to cool completely.

Nutritional Information: Estimated per serving (1 cookie): 140 calories, 4 grams protein, 3 grams carbohydrates, 13 grams fat, 2 grams fiber, 25 milligrams cholesterol, 55 milligrams sodium, 40 milligrams potassium.

Keto Tiramisu

Yield: 6 servings | Prep time: 30 minutes | Cook time: 10 minutes

Ingredients:

For the Ladyfingers:
- 100 grams almond flour
- 4 large eggs, separated
- 50 grams erythritol (or other keto-friendly sweetener)
- 1/2 teaspoon vanilla extract

For the Mascarpone Cream:
- 250 grams mascarpone cheese
- 3 large egg yolks
- 50 grams erythritol (or other keto-friendly sweetener)
- 1/2 teaspoon vanilla extract

For the Coffee Soak:
- 120 milliliters strong brewed coffee, cooled
- 2 tablespoons coffee liqueur (optional, make sure it's keto-friendly)

For Garnish:
- Unsweetened cocoa powder

Directions:

1. Preheat the oven to 180°C (350°F). Line a baking sheet with parchment paper.
2. Make the ladyfingers: In a large bowl, beat the egg whites until stiff peaks form. In another bowl, whisk together the egg yolks, erythritol, and vanilla extract until light and fluffy. Gently fold in the almond flour and egg whites. Pipe or spoon the mixture onto the prepared baking sheet to form ladyfinger shapes. Bake for 8-10 minutes, until lightly golden. Let cool completely.
3. Make the mascarpone cream: In a bowl, beat together the mascarpone cheese, egg yolks, erythritol, and vanilla extract until smooth and creamy.
4. Assemble the tiramisu: Dip the ladyfingers in the coffee mixture and arrange in a single layer in a serving dish. Spread half of the mascarpone cream over the ladyfingers. Repeat with another layer of soaked ladyfingers and mascarpone cream.
5. Cover and refrigerate for at least 4 hours, or overnight, to allow the flavors to meld. Before serving, dust the top with unsweetened cocoa powder.

Nutritional Information: Estimated per serving: 400 calories, 10 grams protein, 5 grams carbohydrates, 38 grams fat, 2 grams fiber, 225 milligrams cholesterol, 150 milligrams sodium, 50 milligrams potassium.

Keto Chocolate Almond Bark

Yield: 6 servings | Prep time: 10 minutes | Cook time: 5 minutes

Ingredients:

- 200 grams unsweetened dark chocolate, chopped
- 100 grams almonds, roughly chopped
- 50 grams erythritol (or other keto-friendly sweetener)
- 1/2 teaspoon vanilla extract
- 1/4 teaspoon sea salt

Directions:

1. Line a baking sheet with parchment paper.
2. In a heat-proof bowl, melt the dark chocolate over a pot of simmering water or in the microwave in 30-second increments, stirring until smooth.
3. Once melted, remove the chocolate from heat and stir in erythritol and vanilla extract until well combined.
4. Stir in half of the chopped almonds, then spread the mixture onto the prepared baking sheet in a thin layer.
5. Sprinkle the remaining almonds and sea salt over the top, pressing them slightly into the chocolate.
6. Place the baking sheet in the refrigerator for at least 1 hour to allow the chocolate to set.
7. Once set, break the bark into pieces and enjoy.

Nutritional Information: Estimated per serving: 210 calories, 5 grams protein, 8 grams carbohydrates, 18 grams fat, 4 grams fiber, 0 milligrams cholesterol, 100 milligrams sodium, 200 milligrams potassium.

Keto Strawberry Shortcake

Yield: 6 servings | Prep time: 20 minutes | Cook time: 15 minutes

Ingredients:

For the Shortcake:
- 200 grams almond flour
- 50 grams coconut flour
- 80 grams erythritol (or other keto-friendly sweetener)
- 2 teaspoons baking powder
- 1/4 teaspoon salt
- 3 large eggs
- 60 milliliters unsweetened almond milk
- 60 milliliters melted coconut oil
- 1 teaspoon vanilla extract

For the Topping:
- 300 grams fresh strawberries, hulled and sliced
- 240 milliliters heavy whipping cream
- 20 grams erythritol (or other keto-friendly sweetener)
- 1/2 teaspoon vanilla extract

Directions:

1. Preheat the oven to 180°C (350°F). Line a muffin tin with paper liners or grease with coconut oil.
2. Make the shortcake: In a bowl, combine the almond flour, coconut flour, erythritol, baking powder, and salt. In another bowl, whisk together the eggs, almond milk, coconut oil, and vanilla extract. Add the wet ingredients to the dry ingredients and mix until well combined. Divide the batter among the prepared muffin cups.
3. Bake for 12-15 minutes, until a toothpick inserted into the center of a shortcake comes out clean. Let cool completely.
4. Make the topping: In a bowl, beat the heavy whipping cream, erythritol, and vanilla extract until stiff peaks form.
5. Assemble the shortcakes: Slice each shortcake in half horizontally. Spoon some of the whipped cream onto the bottom half of each shortcake. Top with strawberries and the remaining shortcake half. Serve immediately.

Nutritional Information: Estimated per serving: 420 calories, 8 grams protein, 9 grams carbohydrates, 40 grams fat, 4 grams fiber, 145 milligrams cholesterol, 210 milligrams sodium, 150 milligrams potassium.

Keto Panna Cotta with Mixed Berries

Yield: 4 servings | Prep time: 15 minutes | Cook time: 5 minutes

Ingredients:

- 400 milliliters full-fat coconut milk
- 4 grams powdered gelatin
- 50 grams erythritol (or other keto-friendly sweetener)
- 1 teaspoon vanilla extract
- 100 grams mixed berries (blueberries, raspberries, strawberries), fresh or frozen
- Optional: zest of 1 lemon

Directions:

1. In a small bowl, sprinkle the gelatin over 3 tablespoons of water and let it sit for about 5 minutes until it softens.
2. In a saucepan, heat the coconut milk over medium heat until it's hot but not boiling. Remove from heat.
3. Add the softened gelatin to the hot coconut milk and whisk until the gelatin is completely dissolved.
4. Add erythritol and vanilla extract and whisk until well combined. Optionally, add lemon zest for extra flavor.
5. Divide the mixture among four dessert cups or ramekins. Place them in the fridge for at least 4 hours, or until the panna cotta is set.
6. Before serving, top each panna cotta with a portion of mixed berries.

Nutritional Information: Estimated per serving: 190 calories, 2 grams protein, 6 grams carbohydrates, 18 grams fat, 1 gram fiber, 0 milligrams cholesterol, 30 milligrams sodium, 120 milligrams potassium.

Keto Chocolate Lava Cake

Yield: 2 servings | Prep time: 10 minutes | Cook time: 12 minutes

Ingredients:

- 50 grams unsweetened dark chocolate, chopped
- 30 grams unsalted butter
- 30 grams erythritol (or other keto-friendly sweetener)
- 1 large egg
- 1 large egg yolk
- 5 grams unsweetened cocoa powder
- 5 grams coconut flour
- 1/4 teaspoon vanilla extract
- Pinch of salt

Directions:

1. Preheat your oven to 220°C (425°F) and grease two ramekins with butter.
2. In a microwave-safe bowl, melt the chocolate and butter together in 20-second intervals, stirring after each interval until smooth.
3. Stir in erythritol until well combined. Add the egg, egg yolk, and vanilla extract and mix until smooth.
4. Add the cocoa powder, coconut flour, and salt to the mixture and stir until well combined.
5. Divide the batter between the prepared ramekins and bake for 10-12 minutes, until the edges are set but the center is still slightly jiggly.
6. Allow the cakes to cool for 1 minute, then run a knife around the edge to loosen. Turn the ramekins onto plates, and serve immediately.

Nutritional Information: Estimated per serving: 290 calories, 8 grams protein, 9 grams carbohydrates, 25 grams fat, 4 grams fiber, 210 milligrams cholesterol, 90 milligrams sodium, 180 milligrams potassium.

Keto Key Lime Pie

Yield: 6 servings | Prep time: 20 minutes | Cook time: 15 minutes

Ingredients:

For the crust:
- 200 grams almond flour
- 45 grams erythritol (or other keto-friendly sweetener)
- 85 grams unsalted butter, melted
- 1/2 teaspoon vanilla extract
- Pinch of salt

For the filling:
- 400 grams cream cheese, softened
- 100 grams erythritol (or other keto-friendly sweetener)
- Zest and juice of 4 key limes (about 60 milliliters juice)
- 1 teaspoon vanilla extract
- 2 large eggs

For the topping:
- 200 milliliters heavy cream
- 2 tablespoons erythritol (or other keto-friendly sweetener)

Directions:

1. Preheat your oven to 180°C (350°F). In a medium bowl, combine almond flour, erythritol, melted butter, vanilla extract, and salt. Press the mixture firmly into the bottom of a 23-cm (9-inch) pie pan. Bake for 10-12 minutes until lightly golden. Remove from the oven and let it cool.
2. In a large bowl, beat cream cheese, erythritol, lime zest, lime juice, and vanilla extract until smooth and creamy. Add eggs one at a time, beating well after each addition. Pour the filling over the crust.
3. Bake for 15 minutes, or until the edges are set but the center is still slightly jiggly. Let the pie cool to room temperature, then refrigerate for at least 4 hours or overnight.
4. Before serving, whip heavy cream and erythritol until stiff peaks form. Spread or pipe onto the pie and garnish with lime zest if desired.

Nutritional Information: Estimated per serving: 490 calories, 11 grams protein, 8 grams carbohydrates, 45 grams fat, 2 grams fiber, 145 milligrams cholesterol, 270 milligrams sodium, 120 milligrams potassium.

Keto Blueberry Muffins

Yield: 6 servings | Prep time: 10 minutes | Cook time: 20 minutes

Ingredients:

- 150 grams almond flour
- 50 grams erythritol (or other keto-friendly sweetener)
- 1/2 teaspoon baking powder
- 1/4 teaspoon salt
- 75 grams unsalted butter, melted
- 2 large eggs
- 1 teaspoon vanilla extract
- 100 grams fresh or frozen blueberries

Directions:

1. Preheat your oven to 180°C (350°F). Line a muffin tin with 6 paper liners.
2. In a large bowl, combine almond flour, erythritol, baking powder, and salt.
3. Add melted butter, eggs, and vanilla extract to the dry ingredients and mix until well combined.
4. Gently fold in the blueberries.
5. Divide the batter evenly among the muffin cups, filling each about 2/3 full.
6. Bake for 18-20 minutes or until a toothpick inserted into the center of a muffin comes out clean.
7. Remove from oven and allow muffins to cool in the pan for 5 minutes before transferring to a wire rack to cool completely.

Nutritional Information: Estimated per serving: 220 calories, 6 grams protein, 7 grams carbohydrates, 19 grams fat, 3 grams fiber, 75 milligrams cholesterol, 110 milligrams sodium, 60 milligrams potassium.

Keto Brownies with Walnuts

Yield: 12 servings | Prep time: 15 minutes | Cook time: 25 minutes

Ingredients:

- 125 grams almond flour
- 30 grams cocoa powder
- 1/2 teaspoon baking powder
- Pinch of salt
- 150 grams erythritol (or other keto-friendly sweetener)
- 115 grams unsalted butter, melted
- 2 large eggs
- 1 teaspoon vanilla extract
- 100 grams dark chocolate (at least 85% cocoa), chopped
- 60 grams walnuts, chopped

Directions:

1. Preheat your oven to 175°C (350°F). Grease a 20-cm (8-inch) square baking pan or line it with parchment paper.
2. In a medium bowl, combine almond flour, cocoa powder, baking powder, and salt. Set aside.
3. In a large bowl, whisk together erythritol, melted butter, eggs, and vanilla extract until well combined. Gradually add the dry ingredients to the wet ingredients, stirring until just combined. Fold in chopped chocolate and walnuts.
4. Pour the batter into the prepared baking pan and smooth the top. Bake for 25 minutes or until a toothpick inserted into the center comes out with a few moist crumbs.
5. Let the brownies cool completely in the pan on a wire rack. Once cooled, cut into 12 squares.

Nutritional Information: Estimated per serving: 200 calories, 5 grams protein, 5 grams carbohydrates, 18 grams fat, 2 grams fiber, 45 milligrams cholesterol, 80 milligrams sodium, 80 milligrams potassium.

Keto Vanilla Custard

Yield: 4 servings | Prep time: 5 minutes | Cook time: 15 minutes

Ingredients:

- 500 millilitres heavy cream
- 1 vanilla pod, split lengthwise, or 1 teaspoon vanilla extract
- 4 large egg yolks
- 30 grams erythritol (or other keto-friendly sweetener)
- A pinch of salt

Directions:

1. In a saucepan, heat the heavy cream and vanilla pod (or extract) over medium heat until it begins to simmer. Remove from heat and allow it to cool slightly. If using a vanilla pod, scrape out the seeds and stir them into the cream.
2. In a separate bowl, whisk together the egg yolks, erythritol, and salt until the mixture is pale and slightly thickened.
3. Gradually add the warm cream to the egg yolk mixture, whisking constantly to prevent the eggs from scrambling. Once fully combined, pour the mixture back into the saucepan.
4. Cook the custard over low heat, stirring constantly, until it thickens enough to coat the back of a spoon. This should take about 10-15 minutes.
5. Remove the custard from heat and strain it through a fine-mesh sieve into a serving dish or individual ramekins. Cover with plastic wrap, making sure the wrap directly touches the surface of the custard to prevent a skin from forming.
6. Chill the custard in the refrigerator for at least 2 hours before serving.

Nutritional Information: Estimated per serving: 420 calories, 5 grams protein, 3 grams carbohydrates, 44 grams fat, 0 grams fiber, 250 milligrams cholesterol, 60 milligrams sodium, 90 milligrams potassium.

Keto Cinnamon Rolls

Yield: 6 servings | Prep time: 20 minutes | Cook time: 25 minutes

Ingredients:

For the Dough:
- 200 grams almond flour
- 55 grams coconut flour
- 30 grams erythritol (or other keto-friendly sweetener)
- 2 teaspoons baking powder
- 1/4 teaspoon salt
- 110 grams unsalted butter, melted
- 2 large eggs

For the Filling:

- 55 grams unsalted butter, melted
- 30 grams erythritol (or other keto-friendly sweetener)
- 2 teaspoons cinnamon

For the Icing:
- 60 grams cream cheese, softened
- 30 grams unsalted butter, softened
- 30 grams erythritol (or other keto-friendly sweetener)
- 1/2 teaspoon vanilla extract

Directions:

1. Preheat your oven to 180°C (350°F). Line a baking sheet with parchment paper or a silicone baking mat.
2. In a large bowl, combine the almond flour, coconut flour, erythritol, baking powder, and salt. Add the melted butter and eggs, and mix until a dough forms.
3. Roll the dough out between two sheets of parchment paper to a rectangle shape, about 30 cm x 20 cm. Remove the top sheet of parchment paper.
4. For the filling, mix together the melted butter, erythritol, and cinnamon in a small bowl. Spread this mixture evenly over the dough. Roll up the dough from the long side, then cut into 6 equal pieces. Place the rolls on the prepared baking sheet.
5. Bake for 25 minutes or until golden brown. Let the rolls cool for a few minutes on the baking sheet.
6. For the icing, beat together the cream cheese, butter, erythritol, and vanilla extract in a small bowl until smooth. Drizzle the icing over the warm cinnamon rolls.

Nutritional Information: Estimated per serving: 370 calories, 9 grams protein, 8 grams carbohydrates, 34 grams fat, 4 grams fiber, 120 milligrams cholesterol, 220 milligrams sodium, 90 milligrams potassium.

Keto Coconut Cream Pie

Yield: 6 servings | Prep time: 15 minutes | Cook time: 20 minutes

Ingredients:

For the crust:
- 200 grams almond flour
- 50 grams coconut flour
- 50 grams unsweetened shredded coconut
- 70 grams butter, melted
- 30 grams erythritol (or other keto-friendly sweetener)
- 1 teaspoon vanilla extract
- A pinch of salt

For the filling:
- 400 millilitres coconut milk
- 4 large egg yolks
- 60 grams erythritol (or other keto-friendly sweetener)
- 1 teaspoon vanilla extract
- 10 grams unflavored gelatine powder
- 250 millilitres heavy whipping cream
- For the topping:
- 50 grams unsweetened shredded coconut, toasted

Directions:

1. Preheat the oven to 180°C (350°F). In a medium-sized bowl, mix together the almond flour, coconut flour, shredded coconut, melted butter, erythritol, vanilla extract, and salt. Press the mixture into the bottom and sides of a pie pan. Bake for 10 minutes until the crust is golden brown. Remove from the oven and allow it to cool.
2. In a saucepan, heat the coconut milk over medium heat until it simmers. In a separate bowl, whisk together the egg yolks and erythritol. Gradually add the warm coconut milk to the egg yolk mixture, whisking constantly. Pour the mixture back into the saucepan.
3. Cook the mixture over low heat, stirring constantly, until it thickens. Remove from heat and stir in the vanilla extract and gelatine powder until well combined.
4. In a separate bowl, whip the heavy cream until stiff peaks form. Gently fold the whipped cream into the coconut milk mixture.
5. Pour the filling into the cooled crust. Sprinkle the toasted shredded coconut on top.
6. Chill the pie in the refrigerator for at least 4 hours before serving.

Nutritional Information: Estimated per serving: 450 calories, 10 grams protein, 8 grams carbohydrates, 42 grams fat, 5 grams fiber, 180 milligrams cholesterol, 90 milligrams sodium, 200 milligrams potassium.

Homemade Keto Snacks for On-the-Go

Keto Almond Joy Bites

Yield: 6 servings | Prep time: 10 minutes | Cook time: 0 minutes (no-bake)

Ingredients:

- 100 grams unsweetened shredded coconut
- 100 grams almond flour
- 50 grams erythritol (or other keto-friendly sweetener)
- 60 millilitres coconut cream
- 1 teaspoon vanilla extract
- 12 whole almonds
- 100 grams dark chocolate (at least 85% cocoa)
- 2 tablespoons coconut oil

Directions:

1. In a medium-sized bowl, combine the shredded coconut, almond flour, erythritol, coconut cream, and vanilla extract. Mix until well combined.
2. Divide the mixture into 12 equal portions and shape them into small balls or ovals. Place one almond on top of each ball and press it gently.
3. Place the balls on a tray lined with parchment paper and refrigerate for at least 30 minutes to firm up.
4. In a small saucepan, melt the dark chocolate and coconut oil together over low heat, stirring until smooth.
5. Once the coconut balls are firm, dip each one into the melted chocolate, ensuring it is completely coated. Place them back onto the parchment paper.
6. Refrigerate for another 30 minutes or until the chocolate has set. Store in an airtight container in the refrigerator.

Nutritional Information: Estimated per serving: 250 calories, 5 grams protein, 8 grams carbohydrates, 22 grams fat, 5 grams fiber, 0 milligrams cholesterol, 25 milligrams sodium, 200 milligrams potassium.

Keto Pork Rinds

Yield: 4 servings | Prep time: 10 minutes | Cook time: 15 minutes

Ingredients:

- 250 grams pork skin, cut into 2-inch squares
- 1 teaspoon sea salt
- 1 teaspoon paprika
- 1 teaspoon garlic powder

Directions:

1. Preheat your oven to 200°C (390°F).
2. Place the pork skin squares on a baking tray lined with parchment paper, making sure they are not overlapping.
3. Sprinkle the pork skin squares with sea salt, paprika, and garlic powder.
4. Bake in the preheated oven for about 15 minutes, or until they are crispy and golden brown.
5. Remove from the oven and let them cool on the baking tray for a few minutes. The pork rinds will continue to crisp up as they cool.
6. Serve immediately or store in an airtight container for up to 2 days.

Nutritional Information: Estimated per serving: 100 calories, 14 grams protein, 0 grams carbohydrates, 5 grams fat, 0 grams fiber, 40 milligrams cholesterol, 600 milligrams sodium, 150 milligrams potassium.

Keto Avocado Hummus

Yield: 4 servings | Prep time: 10 minutes | Cook time: 0 minutes

Ingredients:

- 2 ripe avocados, peeled and pitted
- 150 grams tahini
- 2 tablespoons extra virgin olive oil
- 2 tablespoons lemon juice
- 2 garlic cloves, minced
- 1/2 teaspoon sea salt
- 1/2 teaspoon ground cumin
- 1/4 teaspoon black pepper

Directions:

1. In a food processor, combine the avocados, tahini, olive oil, lemon juice, minced garlic, sea salt, cumin, and black pepper.
2. Process until smooth, scraping down the sides of the bowl as needed. If the hummus is too thick, add a tablespoon of water at a time until the desired consistency is reached.
3. Transfer the hummus to a serving bowl and drizzle with additional olive oil, if desired.
4. Serve with keto-friendly vegetables or keto crackers for dipping.

Nutritional Information: Estimated per serving: 310 calories, 5 grams protein, 8 grams carbohydrates, 30 grams fat, 7 grams fiber, 0 milligrams cholesterol, 300 milligrams sodium, 400 milligrams potassium.

Keto Pizza Rolls

Yield: 4 servings | Prep time: 15 minutes | Cook time: 15 minutes

Ingredients:

- 200 grams mozzarella cheese, shredded
- 100 grams almond flour
- 1 large egg
- 1 teaspoon baking powder
- 1 teaspoon Italian seasoning
- 1/4 teaspoon garlic powder
- 1/4 teaspoon onion powder
- 150 grams keto-friendly marinara sauce
- 100 grams pepperoni slices
- 50 grams black olives, sliced
- 50 grams green bell pepper, thinly sliced
- 50 grams red onion, thinly sliced
- 100 grams cheddar cheese, shredded
- 1 tablespoon olive oil
- 1/2 teaspoon dried basil

Directions:

1. Preheat your oven to 220°C (425°F). Line a baking sheet with parchment paper.
2. In a microwave-safe bowl, combine mozzarella cheese, almond flour, egg, baking powder, Italian seasoning, garlic powder, and onion powder. Microwave for 90 seconds, stirring halfway through.
3. Once the dough has cooled slightly, spread it onto the prepared baking sheet in a rectangular shape. Bake for 10 minutes or until lightly browned.
4. Remove from oven and spread marinara sauce over the dough, leaving a small border around the edges. Top with pepperoni slices, black olives, green bell pepper, red onion, and cheddar cheese.
5. Roll the dough tightly, starting from one of the longer sides. Slice into 8 equal pieces and place them cut-side down on the baking sheet.
6. Brush the tops with olive oil and sprinkle with dried basil. Bake for an additional 5 minutes or until the cheese is melted and bubbly.

Nutritional Information: Estimated per serving: 410 calories, 21 grams protein, 7 grams carbohydrates, 35 grams fat, 3 grams fiber, 95 milligrams cholesterol, 720 milligrams sodium, 300 milligrams potassium.

Keto Parmesan Crisps

Yield: 4 servings | Prep time: 5 minutes | Cook time: 10 minutes

Ingredients:

- 100 grams Parmesan cheese, finely grated
- 1/2 teaspoon garlic powder
- 1/2 teaspoon Italian seasoning
- 1/4 teaspoon black pepper
- 1/4 teaspoon paprika

Directions:

1. Preheat your oven to 180°C (350°F). Line a baking sheet with parchment paper.
2. In a bowl, mix together the grated Parmesan cheese, garlic powder, Italian seasoning, black pepper, and paprika.
3. Spoon tablespoons of the mixture onto the prepared baking sheet, making sure to leave space between each mound.
4. Flatten each mound slightly with the back of the spoon to form a thin, even layer.
5. Bake in the preheated oven for 8-10 minutes or until golden and crisp.
6. Remove from the oven and let cool on the baking sheet for a few minutes before transferring to a wire rack to cool completely.

Nutritional Information: Estimated per serving: 110 calories, 10 grams protein, 1 gram carbohydrates, 7 grams fat, 0 grams fiber, 25 milligrams cholesterol, 430 milligrams sodium, 30 milligrams potassium.

Keto Buffalo Chicken Dip

Yield: 6 servings | Prep time: 10 minutes | Cook time: 20 minutes

Ingredients:

- 450 grams cooked chicken breast, shredded
- 200 grams cream cheese, softened
- 100 grams shredded mozzarella cheese
- 100 grams shredded cheddar cheese
- 120 ml buffalo sauce
- 60 ml ranch dressing
- 1/2 teaspoon garlic powder
- 1/4 teaspoon onion powder
- 1/4 teaspoon black pepper
- 2 green onions, thinly sliced for garnish

Directions:

1. Preheat your oven to 190°C (375°F). Grease a baking dish.
2. In a large bowl, mix together the shredded chicken, cream cheese, mozzarella cheese, cheddar cheese, buffalo sauce, ranch dressing, garlic powder, onion powder, and black pepper until well combined.
3. Transfer the mixture to the prepared baking dish and spread it out evenly.
4. Bake in the preheated oven for 20 minutes or until the dip is bubbly and golden on top.
5. Remove from the oven and let cool slightly before garnishing with sliced green onions.
6. Serve warm with celery sticks, cucumber slices, or other keto-friendly dippers.

Nutritional Information: Estimated per serving: 390 calories, 27 grams protein, 3 grams carbohydrates, 30 grams fat, 0 grams fiber, 120 milligrams cholesterol, 850 milligrams sodium, 200 milligrams potassium.

Keto Garlic Herb Crackers

Yield: 6 servings | Prep time: 10 minutes | Cook time: 12 minutes

Ingredients:

- 200 grams almond flour
- 1/2 teaspoon baking powder
- 1/4 teaspoon salt
- 1/4 teaspoon garlic powder
- 1/4 teaspoon onion powder
- 1 teaspoon dried rosemary
- 1 teaspoon dried thyme
- 1 large egg
- 1 tablespoon olive oil

Directions:

1. Preheat your oven to 180°C (350°F). Line a baking sheet with parchment paper.
2. In a large mixing bowl, combine almond flour, baking powder, salt, garlic powder, onion powder, rosemary, and thyme.
3. In a separate bowl, whisk together the egg and olive oil. Pour the wet ingredients into the dry ingredients and mix until a dough forms.
4. Place the dough between two sheets of parchment paper and roll it out to a thin, even thickness.
5. Remove the top sheet of parchment paper and transfer the rolled-out dough (along with the bottom parchment paper) onto the prepared baking sheet.
6. Using a knife or pizza cutter, score the dough into squares or rectangles.
7. Bake in the preheated oven for 12 minutes or until the crackers are golden brown and crisp.
8. Remove from the oven and let cool before breaking them apart along the scored lines.

Nutritional Information: Estimated per serving: 200 calories, 8 grams protein, 6 grams carbohydrates, 17 grams fat, 3 grams fiber, 30 milligrams cholesterol, 125 milligrams sodium, 100 milligrams potassium.

Keto Cucumber Bites with Smoked Salmon

Yield: 6 servings | Prep time: 10 minutes | Cook time: 0 minutes

Ingredients:

- 1 large cucumber (approximately 300 grams)
- 200 grams smoked salmon
- 100 grams cream cheese
- 1 tablespoon lemon juice
- 1 tablespoon fresh dill, chopped
- 1/2 teaspoon black pepper

Directions:

1. Wash and slice the cucumber into 1.5 cm thick rounds.
2. In a small bowl, combine the cream cheese, lemon juice, dill, and black pepper. Mix until smooth.
3. Spread a small dollop of the cream cheese mixture on top of each cucumber slice.
4. Top each cucumber slice with a small piece of smoked salmon.
5. Garnish with additional fresh dill, if desired.
6. Serve immediately, or refrigerate until ready to serve.

Nutritional Information: Estimated per serving: 90 calories, 8 grams protein, 3 grams carbohydrates, 6 grams fat, 1 gram fiber, 20 milligrams cholesterol, 450 milligrams sodium, 150 milligrams potassium.

Keto Mozzarella Sticks

Yield: 4 servings | Prep time: 15 minutes | Cook time: 6 minutes

Ingredients:

- 200 grams mozzarella cheese, cut into sticks
- 50 grams almond flour
- 2 tablespoons grated parmesan cheese
- 1 teaspoon Italian seasoning
- 1/2 teaspoon garlic powder
- 1/2 teaspoon paprika
- 1/4 teaspoon salt
- 1/4 teaspoon black pepper
- 1 large egg
- 2 tablespoons heavy cream

Directions:

1. In a small bowl, whisk together the egg and heavy cream.
2. In a separate shallow dish, mix together the almond flour, grated parmesan cheese, Italian seasoning, garlic powder, paprika, salt, and pepper.
3. Dip each mozzarella stick into the egg mixture, ensuring it's fully coated, and then roll it in the almond flour mixture, pressing the coating onto the cheese to adhere.
4. Place the coated mozzarella sticks onto a plate lined with parchment paper and freeze for at least 30 minutes.
5. Preheat your air fryer to 190°C (375°F). Cook the frozen mozzarella sticks in the air fryer for about 6 minutes, or until the coating is golden brown and crispy.
6. Serve immediately with your favourite low-carb dipping sauce.

Nutritional Information: Estimated per serving: 225 calories, 12 grams protein, 3 grams carbohydrates, 18 grams fat, 1 gram fiber, 75 milligrams cholesterol, 425 milligrams sodium, 100 milligrams potassium.

Keto Coconut Almond Bars

Yield: 6 servings | Prep time: 10 minutes | Cook time: 0 minutes (No-bake recipe)

Ingredients:

- 100 grams unsweetened shredded coconut
- 75 grams almond flour
- 60 grams unsalted butter, melted
- 30 grams almond butter
- 50 grams erythritol (or other keto-friendly sweetener)
- 1 teaspoon vanilla extract
- 1/4 teaspoon salt
- 50 grams unsweetened dark chocolate, melted for topping
- 25 grams chopped almonds, for topping

Directions:

1. In a medium bowl, combine the shredded coconut, almond flour, melted butter, almond butter, erythritol, vanilla extract, and salt. Mix until well combined.
2. Line a small baking dish (approximately 20 cm x 10 cm) with parchment paper. Transfer the mixture into the lined baking dish and press it down firmly into an even layer.
3. Pour the melted chocolate over the mixture and spread it evenly. Sprinkle the chopped almonds on top.
4. Place the baking dish in the refrigerator for at least 1 hour, or until the bars are set.
5. Remove the baking dish from the refrigerator and lift the bars out of the dish using the parchment paper. Cut the bars into 6 equal pieces.
6. Store the bars in the refrigerator in an airtight container for up to one week.

Nutritional Information: Estimated per serving: 298 calories, 5 grams protein, 8 grams carbohydrates, 28 grams fat, 4 grams fiber, 20 milligrams cholesterol, 100 milligrams sodium, 146 milligrams potassium.

Keto Guacamole and Flaxseed Crackers

Yield: 4 servings | Prep time: 15 minutes | Cook time: 15 minutes

Ingredients:

For the Guacamole:
- 2 ripe avocados, pitted and peeled
- 1 small onion, finely chopped (about 50 grams)
- 1 medium tomato, seeds removed and finely chopped (about 100 grams)
- 1 small jalapeno, seeds removed and finely chopped
- 1 clove garlic, minced
- 1 tablespoon lime juice

- 1/4 teaspoon salt
- 1/4 teaspoon black pepper
- 2 tablespoons fresh coriander, chopped

For the Flaxseed Crackers:
- 150 grams ground flaxseeds
- 1/2 teaspoon salt
- 1/2 teaspoon garlic powder
- 120 millilitres water

Directions:

1. Start by making the guacamole. In a medium bowl, mash the avocados with a fork. Add the onion, tomato, jalapeno, garlic, lime juice, salt, pepper, and coriander. Stir until well combined. Cover and refrigerate until ready to serve.
2. Preheat the oven to 180°C. In a medium bowl, combine the ground flaxseeds, salt, and garlic powder. Add the water and mix until a dough forms. Let the dough sit for a few minutes to thicken.
3. Place the dough between two sheets of parchment paper and roll it out to a thickness of about 2-3 millimetres. Remove the top sheet of parchment paper and cut the dough into crackers using a sharp knife or pizza cutter.
4. Transfer the parchment paper with the crackers onto a baking sheet. Bake in the preheated oven for about 15 minutes, or until the crackers are crisp and golden brown. Allow the crackers to cool completely before breaking them apart.
5. Serve the guacamole with the flaxseed crackers.

Nutritional Information: Estimated per serving: 312 calories, 8 grams protein, 14 grams carbohydrates, 27 grams fat, 11 grams fiber, 0 milligrams cholesterol, 426 milligrams sodium, 528 milligrams potassium.

Keto Greek Tzatziki Dip

Yield: 6 servings | Prep time: 10 minutes | Cook time: 0 minutes

Ingredients:

- 250 grams full-fat Greek yogurt
- 1 medium cucumber (about 150 grams), finely grated and squeezed to remove excess moisture
- 2 cloves garlic, minced

- 2 tablespoons fresh dill, chopped
- 2 tablespoons extra virgin olive oil
- 1 tablespoon lemon juice
- 1/2 teaspoon salt
- 1/4 teaspoon black pepper

Directions:

1. In a medium bowl, combine the Greek yogurt, grated cucumber, minced garlic, chopped dill, olive oil, lemon juice, salt, and pepper. Mix well until all ingredients are fully incorporated.
2. Taste and adjust seasonings, if needed.
3. Cover the bowl with plastic wrap and refrigerate for at least 1 hour, or preferably overnight, to allow the flavours to meld.
4. Serve chilled with keto-friendly vegetables or low-carb bread for dipping.

Nutritional Information: Estimated per serving: 78 calories, 3 grams protein, 3 grams carbohydrates, 6 grams fat, 0 grams fiber, 5 milligrams cholesterol, 213 milligrams sodium, 92 milligrams potassium.

Keto Peanut Butter Cups

Yield: 6 servings | Prep time: 10 minutes | Cook time: 2 minutes

Ingredients:

- 120 grams unsweetened dark chocolate
- 75 grams natural peanut butter (no added sugar)
- 30 grams coconut oil
- 30 grams erythritol (or other keto-friendly sweetener)
- 1/4 teaspoon salt
- 1/4 teaspoon vanilla extract

Directions:

1. In a microwave-safe bowl, melt the chocolate and coconut oil together in 30-second intervals, stirring in between until smooth. Alternatively, you can melt them in a double boiler over low heat.
2. In another bowl, mix the peanut butter, erythritol, salt, and vanilla extract until well combined.
3. Line a muffin tin with 6 paper liners. Spoon a small amount of the melted chocolate into the bottom of each liner and spread it evenly. Freeze for 5 minutes to set.
4. Once set, spoon a dollop of the peanut butter mixture into each cup and spread it out evenly. Top each cup with the remaining melted chocolate, ensuring the peanut butter layer is completely covered.
5. Place the muffin tin in the refrigerator for at least 1 hour, or until the peanut butter cups are set.
6. Remove from the refrigerator and enjoy. Store any leftovers in an airtight container in the refrigerator for up to one week.

Nutritional Information: Estimated per serving: 200 calories, 5 grams protein, 8 grams carbohydrates, 17 grams fat, 3 grams fiber, 1 milligram cholesterol, 85 milligrams sodium, 210 milligrams potassium.

Keto Jalapeno Poppers

Yield: 6 servings | Prep time: 10 minutes | Cook time: 20 minutes

Ingredients:

- 12 jalapeno peppers, halved and seeds removed
- 200 grams cream cheese, softened
- 100 grams cheddar cheese, grated
- 100 grams bacon, cooked and crumbled
- 1 teaspoon garlic powder
- 1/4 teaspoon salt
- 1/4 teaspoon pepper
- 50 grams almond flour
- 2 large eggs, beaten
- 100 grams Parmesan cheese, grated

Directions:

1. Preheat your oven to 180°C (350°F) and line a baking sheet with parchment paper.
2. In a medium-sized mixing bowl, combine the cream cheese, cheddar cheese, crumbled bacon, garlic powder, salt, and pepper. Mix until well combined.
3. Stuff each jalapeno half with the cheese mixture, pressing it down to ensure the filling is compact.
4. Dip each stuffed jalapeno half into the beaten eggs, then roll in a mixture of almond flour and Parmesan cheese. Place them on the prepared baking sheet.
5. Bake for 20 minutes or until the jalapenos are tender and the tops are golden brown.
6. Let them cool for a few minutes before serving.

Nutritional Information: Estimated per serving: 270 calories, 13 grams protein, 5 grams carbohydrates, 22 grams fat, 2 grams fiber, 90 milligrams cholesterol, 420 milligrams sodium, 220 milligrams potassium.

Keto Olive Tapenade with Zucchini Chips
Yield: 4 servings | Prep time: 15 minutes | Cook time: 25 minutes

Ingredients:

For the Olive Tapenade:
- 200 grams pitted Kalamata olives
- 50 grams capers, drained
- 2 garlic cloves, minced
- Zest of 1 lemon
- 2 tablespoons extra virgin olive oil
- 1 tablespoon fresh parsley, chopped
- Salt and pepper to taste

For the Zucchini Chips:
- 2 medium zucchinis, thinly sliced
- 2 tablespoons olive oil
- Salt and pepper to taste

Directions:

1. Olive Tapenade: In a food processor, combine the olives, capers, garlic, lemon zest, olive oil, and parsley. Pulse until the mixture becomes a coarse paste. Season with salt and pepper to taste. Transfer to a bowl and refrigerate until serving.
2. Zucchini Chips: Preheat your oven to 175°C (345°F) and line two baking sheets with parchment paper.
3. Toss the thinly sliced zucchinis with olive oil, salt, and pepper. Lay them out in a single layer on the prepared baking sheets.
4. Bake in the preheated oven for 20-25 minutes or until the zucchini slices become crispy and golden brown. Allow them to cool on the baking sheet for a few minutes before transferring them to a serving plate.
5. Serve the olive tapenade alongside the zucchini chips.

Nutritional Information: Estimated per serving: 190 calories, 2 grams protein, 8 grams carbohydrates, 18 grams fat, 3 grams fiber, 0 milligrams cholesterol, 760 milligrams sodium, 380 milligrams potassium.

Printed in Great Britain
by Amazon